WORLD FAMOUS
HEROES

WORLD FAMOUS HEROES

Giles O'Bryen, Will Hobson and Wynn Wheldon

Constable & Robinson Ltd
3 The Lanchesters
162 Fulham Palace Road
London W6 9ER

This edition published by Magpie Books,
an imprint of Constable & Robinson Ltd 2005

A copy of the British Library Cataloguing in Publication Data
is available from the British Library.

ISBN 1 84529 027 5

Printed and bound in the EU

Contents

Introduction

The Qualities
of a Hero

As far as most of us are concerned, anyone who goes to war and risks his life in battle is a hero. To stand alongside one's fellow soldiers and face up to an enemy intent on causing you injury or death is an act of sufficient courage to earn the admiration and gratitude of those back home, on whose behalf the battle is being fought. The Tomb of the Unknown Soldier stands as a poignant memorial to heroism of this 'ordinary' kind – the kind expected of anyone who calls himself a soldier.

But it is not just in the heat of battle that heroism is required. Throughout history, soldiers have had to endure hardships of many different kinds: long absence from loved ones at home, with all the anxieties that can bring; extreme physical discomfort, caused perhaps by being wet through and bone cold for weeks on end, hunger, thirst, sleep deprivation, the lack of anywhere to rest up and recuperate; alove all, uncertainty – not knowing whether the next day will bring the order to advance and fight, or an enemy attack, or the news that you can pack your bags and go home. A soldier may fire himself up to fight, draw strength from the fellowship of his comrades in arms and take inspiration from the furious maelstrom of battle, but how will he cope with days or weeks of waiting in a temporary shelter far from home, probably cold and hungry, almost certainly tired, and doubtless full of fear about what the future may hold and misgivings about his own ability to do what is required? That requires heroism of an altogether different kind.

Extreme suffering has always been a feature of war and will always remain so. Modern soldiers may be better trained and equipped than their forebears, and they may have access to far superior medical attention if they should be injured, but they face new and deadly threats from violently destructive weapons like battlefield nuclear devices and nerve gas attack from which there is no real defence. Whereas an experienced soldier fighting, for instance, at the Battle of Blenheim in 1704 might have had a good chance of coming out unscathed by sheer force of arms and fighting skill, a modern soldier has no such consolation.

What, then, makes a hero amongst soldiers, a man held in higher esteem even than those prepared to fight and die for a cause or their country? The men whose feats of daring and heroism are described in the following pages have qualities that set them apart: all knew well the dangers they faced (they were brave, not foolish); their achievements by far surpassed what was expected of them, and in many cases proved decisive in the outcome of an engagement; as fighting men they were exceptional either for their strategic and tactical understanding of the nature of war, or simply for their strength and skill; and they were a source of inspiration to their men because their actions gave substance and value to the glory that accrues to those who acquit themselves well in battle – a glory which can too often seem hollow and meaningless to traumatized survivors.

Such men are natural leaders, though often too passionate or impetuous to rise beyond the middle ranks and become great commanders – in this, Alexander the Great and Horatio Lord Nelson are notable exceptions. Whatever their status, their worth to those with whom and for whom they fight is incalculable. For in war, the morale of the fighting men is crucial to success, and crucial to the morale of any fighting force is the inspirational mythology of the war hero, who can provide living proof of the truth of the motto adopted by the British SAS: 'Who Dares Wins'.

Chapter One

Alexander the Great

Alexander the Great, king of Macedonia in the fourth century BC, was the most successful military leader of all time, but it is not his tactical or strategic genius which entitle him to be called a hero. Rather, it is his qualities as a soldier which set him apart: he was possessed of an extraordinary hunger for battle, awesome fortitude and bravery in combat, and a carelessness about his personal safety which, to followers and opponents alike, made him seem like a god.

Alexander was a leader by example – something more or less impossible for a contemporary general because of the dramatic changes in the nature of war that have taken place over the centuries. In Alexander's day, combat was a hand-to-hand affair, and battles could be won or lost according to the outcome of contests between small numbers of out-standing warriors on either side. This facet of war continued right up until the nineteenth century – the retreat of the Napoleonic Guard at Waterloo was the symbolic turning point in the battle – but thereafter the quality and sophistication of military materiel became such that the most potent force available to a commander was more likely to be made of steel than flesh and blood. Of course, small forces of highly trained combat experts such as the SAS or US Marines still play a crucial role in modern warfare, but they tend not to operate in the vanguard of the confrontation between major forces, as they did in Alexander's time. Similarly, you would not expect to see a modern general engaging in a firefight at the spearhead of an advance or manning a Howitzer during an artillery bombardment; and in any century the majority of commanders have preferred to survey the course of events from a safe (and, of course, strategically sensible) distance. But it was once possible for a commander not just to direct a battle, but actually to lead from the front, inspiring those behind him with his prowess, and physically overwhelming any opponent who dared come within range of sword or spear. Such a man was Alexander the Great.

Alexander was the son of Philip of Macedonia, a powerful king but a dissolute man whose tendency to marry any woman who took his fancy contributed much to the turbulence of his reign. Philip himself was a bold and warlike fellow who was reputedly descended from Hercules, so heroic blood ran in Alexander's veins. His mother was a tempestuous woman by the name of Olympias. The day before her marriage to Philip was consummated, she dreamed that her womb was struck by a thunderbolt, after which there was a dazzling explosion of light and a sheet of flame stretched as far as the eye could see. Shortly afterwards, Philip dreamed that he was sealing up his wife's womb, and that on the seal was engraved the figure of a lion. It was further reported that Olympias had been seen asleep with a serpent stretched out at her side. The Macedonians, like other cultures of the time, set great store by such portents, and the circumstances of Alexander's conception – whether by his father, or a thunderbolt, or a god disguised as a snake – could not have been more auspicious. Furthermore, on the day of his birth (20 July 356 BC) the Temple of Artemis at Ephesus was burnt to the ground, and this was widely interpreted as a harbinger of disaster for the established order of things in Asia.

From an early age, Alexander showed both a vehement and impulsive nature, and remarkable powers of self-control. Most striking of all, though, was his thirst for fame and glory – a thirst so strong that in his early teens Alexander dreaded hearing about his father's successes in foreign campaigns because he feared that by the time he came to lead the Macedonian Army there would be nothing left for him to conquer. He had no interest in inheriting a kingdom already rich and far-flung which could provide him with every luxury, but only longed for the chance to prove himself in war.

The story of how Alexander tamed and won the horse Bucephalus shows both his precocious self-assurance, and his courage. He was thirteen at the time – and how many boys of that age would tackle an animal that a body of men who spent their lives training and caring for horses had been unable to touch? Indeed, Alexander's maturity impressed all who met him: perhaps it was that he was being tutored at the time by the philosopher Aristotle (summoned for the task by Philip, who set far greater store by learning than his son did); or perhaps it was simply that Alexander had never once doubted that his future lay in seeking glory on the field of battle, and so all his energies were directed to that end.

By the time he was sixteen, Philip was accustomed to leaving Alexander in charge of his kingdom while he went off on military campaigns to subdue this or that part of the kingdom, or conquer new territories. And it appears that Macedonia was kept in better order by the son than by the father, for when Philip died, the factions engendered by his lifetime of amorous liaisons were feuding openly, the Greek states he had defeated in battle were far from ready to submit to his authority, and neighbouring barbarian tribes were alert to the slightest opportunity to throw off the rule of Macedonia and install their own kings instead. The kingdom Alexander inherited at the age of twenty did not look much like one which could support an extended military campaign.

Alexander & Bucephalus

The story is told of how a visitor from Thessaly offered to sell Philip a fine horse named Bucephalus. The king and his friends went down to the plains to watch the horse being put through its paces, but the beast proved totally unmanageable, refusing to let any of its handlers or the king's grooms come near it. The king grew impatient, and turned to leave but was confronted by Alexander muttering irritably that none of the grooms knew how to handle the horse and as a result an opportunity to buy a magnificent animal would go to waste. Philip and Alexander then struck a bargain: if Alexander could manage the horse, he would have it; if not, he would have to pay for it. Alexander quickly approached Bucephalus and turned the horse towards the sun, for he had noticed that it was shying at its own shadow. He ran alongside the horse for a while, then jumped lightly on its back. At first Bucephalus charged off full of indignance that this small boy should take such a liberty, but Alexander's deft, gentle hands soon won him round, and they galloped back in high style to where Philip and his retinue were waiting. Alexander's performance was greeted with loud applause, and when he had dismounted Philip kissed him and said: 'My boy, we must find you a kingdom big enough for your ambitions. Macedonia is too small for you!'

Statue of Aristotle

Heroes

But Alexander was impatient to begin his quest for glory. His advisers warned him not to risk direct confrontation with restless states in his kingdom, but the young king decided to do exactly the reverse, and mounted an expeditionary force to attack the city of Thebes. There was nothing very heroic about the sack which followed – Alexander put it down to the need to make an example so terrible that none of the states would dare oppose him again, but the massacre of the Thebans was excessively cruel even by the standards of the day. Alexander himself seems to have been haunted by guilt over the atrocity, and of those Thebans who survived, any who came to him with a request were granted whatever they asked for. Perhaps he was over-impatient to prove himself, or too inexperienced to judge the distinction between severity and barbarity, but whatever the reason Alexander never again perpetrated such a wanton and bloodthirsty act.

Alexander was now free to pursue his fate, and set off on a campaign of glorious conquest which would make him famous to the very edges of the known world. His army by this time numbered some 43,000 infantry and 6,000 cavalry – a formidable force, but by no means large by comparison with the armies hundreds of thousands strong which could be mustered by the neighbouring Persians. Furthermore, his men had barely enough supplies to last thirty days. Before his departure, Alexander had parcelled out most of his property and lands to friends and relatives who could look after them during what he evidently expected to be a lifelong absence from his home country. But in sloughing off his responsibilities, he had also handed over the income that went with them and would have nothing to fall back on if times turned hard in the months ahead. It must have been hard to keep up the morale of his fighting men under such circumstances. Though not entirely unproven, Alexander had no experience in leading a prolonged military campaign, during which they would certainly have to face both powerful enemies bent on their destruction and many unexpected perils as well. Unless they won a substantial victory within the first month of their campaign, they would either starve, or have to return home with their tails between their legs. And what was it all for? The greater glory of Alexander . . . To some the expedition was imbued with the spirit of heroic adventure, but to others it must have looked like the folly of an arrogant young man who had spent too long buried in the fantastical exploits of Odysseus in the *Iliad*. Alexander never failed to take a copy of Homer's epic poem wherever he went, and numbered it as one of his most prized possessions.

Yet the army took a chance on Alexander. Few are blessed with unqualified self-belief, and those who are seem to have formed a brilliant alliance with their own destiny – they look like people worth following. Alexander is said to have had fair skin with a ruddy tinge, golden hair and a lithe, graceful bearing, and to his rough-hewn soldiers he must have seemed like one of the statues of gods they had seen in the temples at home. And there were those rumours about his otherworldly parentage, about how Philip had refused to sleep with Olympias because he feared she might be a consort of the gods . . . Whatever you believed about him, Alexander had another quality the Greeks gave a name to: charisma.

The expeditionary force crossed the Hellespont into what is now Turkey, and Alexander went to offer the ritual sacrifices to Athena at Troy, then paid tribute to the tomb of Achilles. This done, he was ready for war.

The Persian kingdom into which Alexander had trespassed was under the rule of Darius III. His kingdom was vast and rich, and upon hearing news of Alexander's intentions he had quickly been able to muster an army far greater than his opponent's. His generals took up a position on the eastern banks of the River Granicus, guarding the only place where the waters were quiet and shallow enough to be safely crossed, and thus effectively barring Alexander's way. The Macedonian generals considered the position impregnable, and said so to Alexander: to take an army across a large river was a challenge in itself; to do so in the face of a powerful enemy would be the height of folly, especially since the terrain on the eastern banks, where they would have to throw back the Persian front lines, was composed of a steep bank of slippery rocks and mud, not at all well suited to a fierce cavalry charge. Furthermore, there was an old tradition according to which Macedonian kings never went to war in the month of *Daesius* (May/June – harvest time in this part of the world). All in all, the wise heads amongst Alexander's entourage were very much against any rash moves against the Persians at this early stage in the campaign.

Alexander's response was to rename the month *Artemisius* after Artemis, the Goddess of War, and declare that the Hellespont would blush for shame if, once he had crossed it, he should shrink back before so feeble a torrent as the Granicus. He then immediately mounted Bucephalus, ordered the attack to begin, and plunged into the river with thirteen squadrons of cavalry, advancing through the flood under a hail of missiles from the astonished Persians, who had been expecting a series of lengthy manoeuvres. Many of his men and horses were swept off their feet and carried away by the surging waters, but Alexander reached the other side, and immediately became embroiled in a fierce hand-to-hand battle with the enemy, who charged with spears lowered, then drew their swords when their first blows had struck home.

The young king had got so far ahead of his men that it was a matter of minutes before they could join him. The odds were very much against him surviving the assault, but

Alexander was in his element, matching the yells of the Persian cavalry with his own warlike shouts, and slashing or thrusting with his sword at any who came within reach. His breastplate was pierced by a Persian javelin, but Alexander smashed the weapon from his opponent's grip and thrust his own blade into the man's throat. Soon there seemed to be a little more space around the king as those who had engaged him first were struck to the ground or forced to give way under the power and ferocity of his attack. As Bucephalus pawed the ground, snorted and reared with hooves lashing out – the great horse every bit as eager for the fray as his rider – it already looked as if Alexander, far from being in mortal danger himself, was now a mortal danger to all who came near him. To the soldiers following behind him, the sight of their leader single-handedly hurling back the Persian assault and laying claim to a few precious square yards of enemy soil must have been one to gladden the hearts of the most phlegmatic amongst them, and they redoubled their efforts to rally to his side.

In case there was any doubt about the identity of this bold warrior and the huge and furious warhorse who carried him into battle, Alexander carried a distinctive shield, and wore a tall, white plume on either side of his helmet. As his cavalry surged towards him, two Persian officers with ambitions to claim a famous scalp decided to hazard a charge at the Macedonian king. Seeing them coming, Alexander lowered his lance and, evading the spear thrust of the one, struck the other on his breastplate. The lance snapped, so Alexander drew his sword once more and struck out at his opponent. But in the meantime the other officer had got behind him and, rising in his stirrups, brought down a battleaxe with all his strength on Alexander's head. The blow split the crest of his helmet, sheared away one of the plumes and grazed the top of Alexander's head. Badly dazed, the king struck out desperately with his sword and cut down his first opponent, then wheeled Bucephalus around to face the attack but only in time to see the axe raised high for a second stroke. To all who watched it seemed as if only the intervention of the gods could have saved Alexander from the first blow; now he must surely die. But at this moment the doughty shape of 'Black' Cleitus, commander of the Royal Squadron of Companion Cavalry, breasted the slope of the river bank and thundered across the broken ground towards his king, lance lowered and aimed straight and true. The axe seemed to hesitate in the air before beginning its downward arc, then the bloodied weapon tumbled from his hands as Cleitus's spear shunted the Persian officer from his horse, the freshly sharpened tip driving abruptly through armour, bone and flesh.

With his Companion Cavalry at his side, Alexander's charge took on a new and unstoppable impetus which broke the back of Persian resistance in this part of the battle-field, and made an apparently invincible army look weak and vulnerable. As so often with the heroic cavalry charges Alexander loved to lead, it was not just the decimation inflicted on his opponents which made his actions so significant, but the effect he had on their morale was also crucial. With breathtaking speed and driven by uncompro-mising self-belief, Alexander had made victory possible in a situation which should have been hopeless, and the enemy, once comfortable in the knowledge that victory would be theirs, suddenly had to face the prospect of inglorious defeat. No wonder the sight of Alexander at the head of a cavalry charge spread panic amongst his intended victims.

The other advances which Alexander had ordered before his fateful plunge into the Granicus had occurred more or less simultaneously, but were faring less well. Assailed by the cream of the Persian cavalry, the Macedonians to the left and right of Alexander were initially unable to make headway. But by absorbing the momentum of the enemy

Dressing for Battle

Alexander had a number of favoured items which he liked to put on before battle. He wore a tunic made in Sicily, which he belted at the waist, and over this a thickly quilted linen corselet captured at the Battle of Issus. His helmet was the work of the master armourer Theophilus, and was made of steel which gleamed like polished silver, and fitted with a gorget studded with precious stones. He also sported an ornate cloak made by the artist Helicon, an item of some antiquity and considerable value when it was presented to him by the city of Rhodes. The sword he carried was a gift from the king of Citium and was a marvel of lightness and tempering – the weapon was so effective that he trained himself to use it as his principal armament in hand-to-hand fighting, in preference to the more usual thrusting weapons, which were brutal but cumbersome.

Alexander always rode Bucephalus into battle, but as the warhorse grew old, he was spared service during the tedious business of reviewing the soldiers and drawing up battle phalanxes, when Alexander rode a reserve horse.

Alexander was clearly well aware of the effect his appearance could have on his men and his enemies, especially in the days when the ornate, showy items he favoured were rare and exceptionally valuable.

charge and creating bridgeheads on the east bank of the river, they had done enough to give Alexander's brilliant attack a chance to succeed. Once it had done so, the tables were turned. The Macedonian cavalry – armed with lances of cornel wood which were considerably more effective than the light javelins of their opponents – were eventually able to take up their favoured wedge formation, and from then on their superiority soon told. The Persian lines were broken in several places, and the cavalry fled in disorder. The Macedonian infantry were now able to follow the horsemen across the river, and the full might of Alexander's army, with the scent of blood and glory in their nostrils, was unleashed upon the hapless Persian infantry. They put up little resistance, with the exception of a detachment of Greek mercenaries, who took up a defensive position and sent out a message requesting an armistice. But in the heat of battle, Alexander was in no mood to parley, and a massacre ensued. The Macedonian king moved quickly to capture the Persian baggage and secure the surrounding area, and the rout was complete.

The battle, and Alexander's part in it, illustrates why heroism has always been so important in war: armies and fighting men are almost certain to find themselves from time to time in circumstances which seem to offer no hope of escape, and an act of great courage and daring can have a near-miraculous effect, taking the enemy by surprise and giving the soldiers a rallying point and a source of hope and inspiration where previously there was none.

The disaster for the Persians was complete. What had seemed like an unassailable defensive position had, with ominous rapidity, been overwhelmed by a small force of cavalry with a young man who fought like a god at their head. Their finest cavalry and the bulk of their infantry had been utterly decimated, and there was nothing now to prevent Alexander taking control of the whole of Asia Minor.

Conscious of the scale of the defeat and its implications for the kingdom, the senior surviving Persian general went home and committed suicide. Alexander paid due tribute to the goddess Athene, buried his dead with full honours, and set about asserting his authority over his new lands.

Though impatient to continue his march inland, Alexander knew it would be prudent first to secure the Mediterranean coast and do what he could to ensure that the major cities in the region would not turn against him once he had ventured further east. However, while in Cilicia (what is now southern Turkey) he fell dangerously ill, and his physicians dared not treat him for fear that he would die under their care. Only one, called Philip, thought it shameful not to use all the resources of his art to help Alexander back to health. But while Philip was treating him, the king received a letter warning him that Darius had offered the physician a large sum of money to poison his patient. It so happened that he received the letter on the day Philip intended to prepare a powerful medicine, which would either cure the king, or it might kill him. Alexander hid the letter and showed it to no one, until the appointed hour when Philip arrived bearing the potion in a large cup. Alexander handed Philip the letter, then took the cup and drank it down as Philip read. Though alarmed by its contents, the physician was reassured by Alexander's face, which displayed his friendship and trust. But as the draught took effect Alexander fell back in a swoon and showed hardly any signs of life. Philip worked desperately to restore his patient to consciousness, and eventually Alexander came round. Shortly afterwards he left his tent to show himself to his men, who would not rest or be consoled until they had seen their king alive.

This sickness, along with the tedious business of securing his authority as far south as Syria, had taken many months and Darius III had wasted no time in mustering a second and even larger army with which to pursue the intruder and drive him back across the Hellespont. The army he now marched down to Cilicia was reputed to number 600,000 men, and though this figure is no doubt an exaggeration, Darius's force did vastly outnumber Alexander's; perhaps more significantly, Darius had managed to muster 30,000 Greek mercenaries and a large contingent of cavalry. All contemporary observers agreed that the Macedonians were about to be crushed.

Though Darius had been warned that Alexander, far from taking fright at so powerful an army, would move to attack him as soon as possible, the Persian king believed otherwise. During the manoeuvres which followed, as each commander jockeyed for the position which would best exploit his own strengths and expose any weakness in the enemy line-up, Darius found himself hemmed in between the mountains and the sea, in a position which meant that only a small proportion of his vast force could be brought to bear on Alexander's men at any one time. Alexander saw that the moment was right, and pounced.

Once again, the main attack was launched by Alexander at the head of the Royal Squadron of Companion Cavalry, and once again he carried them into battle with such vehemence and fury that the Persian infantry who faced him were unable to withstand the shock of this whirlwind attack and the famous plumed helmet pierced deep into the Persian formations. The heavily armed horsemen behind opened up a wedge into which the Macedonian infantry phalanx were intended to march, but again Alexander and his cavalry had thrust forward so fast and furiously that the footmen were in danger of getting left behind. The invincible reputation of the Macedonian infantry phalanx seemed to be under dire threat – bogged down and isolated, and under attack from the flank, where the particular formation they had taken up was at its weakest.

It seemed impossible that Alexander could do anything to help them. However, his charge had inevitably found the weakest point in the Persian defence, and – to the Macedonian king's delight – he now found himself within sight of a cluster of exceptionally large and well-armed soldiers surrounding a magnificent chariot in which stood the tall, stately figure of Darius himself. Driving Bucephalus on with renewed gusto, Alexander and a handful of the Companion Cavalry managed to engage Darius and his personal guard in hand-to-hand combat.

Drawing his beloved sword, Alexander came up along-side Darius's chariot and struck out at the Persian king. Eyes glittering with the ecstasy of battle, the great horse pounding the dust beneath him, blade slicing the air, Alexander must have been a terrifying sight; but Darius was himself a brave man and a seasoned soldier, and did not flinch from the fight. His rage at the Macedonian must have been great, and no doubt the prospect of a possible further humiliation at his hands gave an extra edge to his thrusts and blows. At any rate, as the two leaders clashed the issue was being decided elsewhere: the Companions, pouring down upon the Persian guard in ever greater numbers, had thoroughly mastered them, and Darius must either fight alone or flee. He chose the latter course, but not before he had managed to wound Alexander in the thigh – an injury which the Macedonian king later wrote off as a pinprick.

Observing Darius's flight, the Persian infantry in the vicinity decided that their cause was lost, and began a retreat which eased the pressure on the Macedonian infantry phalanx further to the left. Alexander's own charge was far from over, and he continued to lead the Companions in the direction of the phalanx, all of which allowed them time to regroup and mount a counter-offensive against the large contingent of Darius's mercenaries which had come so close to destroying them. News of Darius's flight had by now reached the outer wings of the Persian force, and Alexander's right, which consisted of a contingent of Thessalians under the command of Parmenion, chose this moment to attack. Finding themselves in retreat on all sides, the Persian army gave way to panic, and began to flee in confusion.

The vast size of Darius's army, which had been of no help during the battle, was a cruel hindrance in defeat. Hemmed in on all sides, the infantry could not escape from the bottleneck fast enough, and the cavalry, the last of the army to turn and run, had to plunge through the mass of footmen to make good their escape. Alexander's forces kept up their attack until nightfall, and the massacre must have been dreadful to see.

For the second time in less than a year, a massively superior Persian force had been routed from what had looked like an impregnable position. And again, the catalyst for the change in fortunes had been a searing cavalry charge led by the young King Alexander, risking his own life in a daring action which had the effect of knocking back the Persian lines, destroying their morale, and relieving the near-intolerable pressure on his own men in another part of the battlefield. Alexander could not have known how significant his personal bravery would be: he led the heroic charge because it was in his nature to do so, and he overwhelmed his opponents because of his own skill and strength and those of his cavalry – and also because he never doubted that he would do so.

For Darius, the humiliation of a further military loss of unimaginable proportions was compounded when Alexander, moving to take the Persian baggage trains in the rear of their positions, also captured the Persian king's wife, mother and daughters. Though Alexander treated them with exaggerated respect – anxious to impress upon his own men as much as upon his enemies that the pleasures of the flesh were beneath him – for a man as proud as Darius the knowledge that his womenfolk were at the mercy of the man who had twice mastered him on the battlefield and was now busy dismembering his kingdom must have been unendurable.

Alexander turned again to the more mundane business of securing his authority over the states that bordered the eastern Mediterranean. A series of lengthy sieges sapped the morale of his men and made Alexander restless, and he lost no chance to lead detachments of soldiers on missions to subdue troublesome states and tribes. On one such adventure he was accompanied by his tutor Lysimachus, who had insisted on joining his pupil on an attack on an Arab force in the Lebanon because he claimed he was neither older nor weaker than Achilles's tutor Phoenix (this explanation gives an indication of how seriously Alexander and his entourage took the example of the great heroes of the past). Unfortunately, when the force entered mountainous territory and had to leave their horses and climb the slopes on foot, Lysimachus soon became exhausted and began to lag behind. Since they were by then approaching the enemy camp and darkness was falling, Alexander refused to leave his tutor's side. Before long the two men, along with a handful of soldiers, found themselves separated from the main force. It was a bitterly cold night, and the rough mountain slopes offered no hope of shelter. Just as his party were beginning to despair and give themselves up as lost, Alexander spotted in the distance a scattering of fires on the outposts of the enemy encampment. Knowing that his men needed something to boost their spirits, Alexander dashed down to the nearest campfire, killed the two Arabs who were sitting by it, then ran back bearing a firebrand. They quickly built up a large fire, and stood ready to defend themselves from the attack which would surely follow. But the Arabs had been so awed by the sight of the Macedonian king rushing into their midst as if they were no more than a bunch of old washerwomen that the majority of them thought it prudent to wait until morning before making an attack, and the few who did venture into the mountains were quickly dispatched by Alexander and his men. They were thus able to spend the night in relative safety and rejoin the main force at dawn the following day.

Alexander's campaign of conquest continued as far south and west as Egypt and to the east almost to the gates of Babylon. In the meantime, Darius was making overtures towards the Macedonian king, offering him money and lands if he would call off his campaign. In one famous incident, Alexander was discussing Darius's latest offer with his advisers. After seeing the terms suggested, Parmenion said: 'I would accept those terms if I were Alexander.' Alexander's retort was crushing: 'So would I, by Zeus, if I were Parmenion!' His response to Darius was an unqualified rejection of any terms that fell short of total surrender, and left Darius little choice but to try to raise a third army with which to repel the invasion of his lands. After a vigorous campaign of enlistment, concentrated in the eastern part of his kingdom which Alexander was yet to conquer, the Persian king mustered an army which has been estimated at 100,000 infantry and 34,000 cavalry. Having seen the havoc wrought by Alexander's Companion horsemen at Granicus and Issus, Darius had ensured that his cavalry outnumbered his opponent's by five to one, and he had also taken steps to ensure that their weapons were stronger and heavier. A new royal guard of elite fighting men had been recruited to serve directly under Darius, and they would be further buttressed by the remnants of the Greek mercenaries. Darius also had perhaps 200 scythed chariots and a small contingent of elephants amongst his forces. The line-up was, if anything, even more formidable than at Issus, although his infantry remained dependent on sheer weight of numbers, and were no match for the better armed and trained and much more experienced men under Alexander's command.

The two great armies marched towards each other and took up positions on the plain of Gaugamela. For some time they scouted each other's positions and assessed each other's strengths and weaknesses, the Macedonians growing increasingly nervous as the overwhelming superiority of Darius's forces became apparent. Alexander's advisers reported their concerns to him and recommended that he attack by night so as to disguise from his own men the extent of the odds against them. The king's response was curt: 'I will not steal my victory.' Alexander was eager to defeat Darius in broad daylight, depriving the Persian king of any excuse for failure – and perhaps his instincts were correct: it would take many years and many more battles before the resources of his opponent were exhausted, but if Darius were to lose heart then all his lands would quickly fall under Alexander's control.

Alexander was reported to have slept exceptionally soundly on the night before the battle, and also to have spent much time carrying out mysterious rituals and sacrifices in the company of his chief diviner, who was called Aristander. At dawn he drew his troops up into battle formation: as was by now his custom, Alexander took control of the right, with Parmenion on the left and the infantry phalanx at the centre. In response, Darius placed his strongest forces on his left, in order to counter the expected attack from the Companion Cavalry.

Initially, Alexander was outflanked by the powerful force of Bactrian cavalry which had been pitted against him, but he was ready for this and moved his men to the right, so that the Persians were forced back to the centre. Though

The Study of Heroism

Alexander took the business of heroism very seriously, and his acts of daring and bravery were seldom carried out on the spur of the moment. At the Battle of Issus, the most precious item captured was a beautifully wrought casket made of gold and silver and encrusted with jewels. Alexander used the casket to contain one of his own most valued possessions – his copy of Homer's epic of heroes and heroism, the *Iliad*.

His attitude to his own heroic ancestors combined reverence and competitiveness in equal measure. Greek and Macedonian heroes were frequently elevated to the kind of status enjoyed, for instance, by Christian saints, and Alexander never lost an opportunity to offer an appropriate sacrifice when he found himself at the scene of a heroic triumph or tragedy. At other times he went out of his way to succeed where past heroes had failed: in Egypt he crossed a desert which was reputed to have claimed the lives of an army of 50,000 men, simply to sacrifice at the shrine of a god he believed to be a local manifestation of Zeus; and while in India he besieged and captured a citadel perched in a seemingly impregnable position 8,000 feet up Mount Aornus – the stronghold was of no real strategic importance, but it had been reported to him that Heracles had once tried and failed to capture it. As the historian Plutarch put it, 'the proud spirit which he carried into all his endeavours had instilled in him a passion for overcoming obstacles.'

they tried to counteract the movement, their ranks were massed too deeply for a rapid redeployment, and Alexander's Companions inexorably swept towards the extreme left of the Persian lines. Over on the Macedonians' right, these manoeuvres were bringing more and more forces to bear on Parmenion and his troops, whose function it was to hold firm and take the brunt of the attack while Alexander probed for a weakness in the Persian lines.

It was a hot, dry day, and as the horses' hooves pounded and pawed at the earth, a thick cloud of dust began to form over the entire battlefield. The shouted orders and responses mingled with curses of frustration and warlike yells as the two huge forces ground against each other like two wrestlers trying each other's strength before finally coming to grips. Alexander's horsemen moved steadily left, and the tension rose to breaking point as both armies waited for the moment when the king would unleash them and attempt the breakthrough that would decide the outcome of the battle.

The Persian left now wheeled to avoid being outflanked themselves and engaged a detachment of mercenaries to Alexander's right. At the same time, Darius launched what should have been a lethal chariot charge at Alexander's cavalry but they were met instead by a force of light infantry who swarmed in amongst the heavy chariots, dodging the whirling blades at their wheels and despatching horse and driver alike with hurled javelins. Few got through to the Macedonian lines, which opened to allow them to pass harmlessly through to the rear. More and more Persian forces were now drawn over to the battle raging on the extreme right, and the lines in front of Alexander were weakening. It was the moment Alexander had been waiting for.

Spurring his men on with an invocation to Zeus, he hurled Bucephalus at the heart of the Persian defences, cracking open the enemy position and exposing their massed infantry to the heavy lances of the cavalry while the phalanx behind rolled thunderously into the breach, knocking back the Persians like a giant battering ram. Up ahead, Alexander carried his Royal Squadron straight through the heart of the Persian centre, sending Darius into headlong flight. Once again, the charge was so violent and ferocious that it carried Alexander's contingent far ahead of the rest, and for a while there was a danger that the Macedonian line would be broken on the left, where Parmenion was still stoutly resisting the heavy assault thrown against him and where a gap had been left by the forward movement of the phalanx. But once news of the destruction of the centre filtered through the dust and reached the Persian right, their spirit was broken. The familiar pattern of Alexander's battles had repeated itself again: by personally leading a make-or-break assault on enemy positions, the Macedonian king had relieved pressure on his forces right across the battlefield, and destroyed the morale of the enemy.

These were not just the actions of a strategic genius or a man with a born soldier's feel for the practicalities of battle, these were exploits as daring and courageous as any in the history of warfare.

Alexander fully expected Darius to raise another army against him if he could and was therefore determined to capture the Persian king. However, the vacuum left by the third defeat of the Persians had to be filled, and with his newly won empire now stretching – in theory at least – across the whole of Asia Minor, Alexander's time was fully occupied by the need to subdue an uprising here, besiege a city there, or install an administration that would both remain loyal to him and popular with its subjects. To achieve such tasks, Alexander was forced to divide his forces, and no further set-piece battles were fought until the campaign in India was under way.

Sharing Hardships

The final pursuit of Darius, following his capture by the Bactrian leader Bessus, took place across the hot, dry and mountainous landscape of what is now northern Afghanistan and Pakistan. At one point his men had covered nearly 400 miles in eleven days, and many were on the verge of collapse from thirst. Alexander himself was almost fainting under the heat of the midday sun when they came across a party of tribesmen bearing water to their camp. They saw the state Alexander was in, and quickly filled a helmet with water and gave it to him; but when the king looked up and saw the haggard faces of his men craning their necks for a sight of the water, he handed it back without drinking a drop. He thanked the men who had offered it, but said: 'If I am the only one to drink, the rest will lose heart.'

No sooner had his troops witnessed this act of self-denial for their sakes than they shouted out for him to lead them on wherever he would, for they could never feel hunger or thirst or any of the weaknesses to which mortal men are subject so long as they had such a king.

By the spring of 330 BC Darius had indeed succeeded in raising a small army of perhaps 9,000 men, one-third of them cavalry. However, he could no longer rely on the support of all the tribes and states of his former empire, and many powerful local leaders were beginning to intrigue against him. Meanwhile, Alexander learned that his old foe had mustered his army in the city of Ecbatana, and set off in hot pursuit. But as he approached the city he discovered that Darius had left five days earlier, marching east towards Bactria. Alexander reduced his pursuing army to an elite corps of 20,000 of his finest fighting men, left the rest under the charge of Parmenion, and set off on a forced march.

It looked like the end of Darius's reign was drawing near, and his supporters were abandoning him in droves. The king's downfall was complete when Bessus, leader of the Bactrians, had him arrested and thrown in chains. Alexander drew ever closer, paring down his forces to 6,000 mounted men for the final push, but when they finally burst into the Persian camp, they found Darius lying in the back of a wagon, riddled with javelins and on the point of death. Alexander gave him a full ceremonial funeral, and later had Bessus brutally killed for his ill-treatment and murder of the man who had once been known as the 'Great King'.

Rather than a single, centralized power capable of raising a large army to throw against him, Alexander now found himself having to subdue smaller forces mustered by individual states eager to exploit the turmoil created by the collapse of Darius's empire. A campaign of sieges and skirmishes followed, with Alexander the strategist showing the speed of thought and ability to improvise which is the hallmark of genius, and Alexander the soldier ever ready to throw himself into the heat of battle at the head of his troops. His habit of fighting his way far ahead of the main body of his men several times brought him to the point of death, and he received wounds in the leg, shoulder, neck and head, the last of which for a time rendered him near speechless. On one occasion he pursued a tribe of Saca nomads whom he had just defeated in battle for ten miles, despite suffering from an attack of dysentery and the after-effects of a head wound. But such injuries only increased

Alexander discovering the body of Darius

Heroes

Alexander's appetite for war, and he became ever more impatient to bring the states and provinces of Asia Minor to heel so that he could continue his grand campaign of conquest in the east.

By the spring of 327 BC, Alexander felt sufficiently secure to begin his march on India. The crossing of the River Indus was a significant moment for the Macedonian king, representing the symbolic completion of his campaign in Asia Minor, and the start of what he hoped would be an even more glorious campaign of conquest in India and beyond. He celebrated the crossing with lavish sacrifices and athletic games, and was fêted by the local prince, Omphis, who arrived to pay homage with an impressive contingent of thirty elephants.

At first Alexander encountered only token resistance from small forces which tended to scatter into the hills at the sight of his heavily armed cavalry and formidable infantrymen. However, one prince, who commanded a sizeable territory reputedly numbering 300 towns, refused to be cowed, and took up a defensive position on the banks of the River Hydaspes. The main strength of his army was a formidable division of elephants, the largest of which the prince – himself a man of six feet three inches – was accustomed to riding into battle. The prince, whose name was Porus, hoped to neutralize Alexander's famed cavalry by lining up his elephants along the river bank in full view of the warhorses, which could never be persuaded to cross the water under the gaze of such terrifying beasts. Alexander's response was to divide his forces into two, leaving the larger contingent to carry out threatening manoeuvres opposite Porus's lines, while he secretly led a smaller force of his finest cavalry and infantry (perhaps 6,000 of each) to a crossing point further up the river.

Once across, Alexander led an advance guard of cavalry against a detachment of Indian horsemen led by one of

Porus's sons, and the predictable rout followed. Porus now wheeled his main force to face the Macedonians, placing elephants at frequent intervals to deter cavalry attack, and filling the gaps with infantry. It was a logical position to take up, but Alexander, in charge of a small, mobile force of elite fighting men and with glorious conquest once again his aim, was in his element. The phalanx was allowed to advance at a leisurely pace in the centre, while Alexander galloped magisterially across to the right with his Companion Cavalry sweeping along behind. Elephants notwithstanding, the sight of the warlike Macedonian king and his invincible cavalry preparing for battle must have brought a shiver to the spine of all those who witnessed it. Alexander began by commanding his mounted archers to fire into the Indian left and then, exploiting the resulting confusion, he drove deep into their flank. Having already suffered one defeat at his hands, the Indian cavalry were in no mood to put up a heroic resistance now. Reinforcements were summoned from the Indian right, but Alexander's momentum could not be stopped, and when the horsemen on the Macedonian left also attacked, the Indian cavalry on both sides began to retreat into the infantry lines in the centre. Porus had little option now but to order his elephants and infantry to take on the Macedonian phalanx. But adapting a tactic used to absorb the scythed chariot attack at Gaugamela, the phalanx parted to allow the animals to lumber through; the Macedonians then used their long spears, or *sarisae*, to dislodge the riders and drive the animals back into their own lines. For a time, confusion reigned, but with Alexander and his triumphant cavalry encircling from the rear and the phalanx showing the greater discipline in the centre, the outcome of the battle was never in doubt. Porus showed the utmost bravery in defeat, refusing to be dislodged from his elephant and fighting on until his army had left the field and he himself was wounded. Hugely impressed by the way the gigantic Indian prince had handled himself in battle, Alexander treated him with the utmost generosity – which he could well afford to do since Porus's army had been annihilated. The only source of sorrow amidst the general rejoicing was the loss of Alexander's trusty old warhorse Bucephalus.

This was to be the one and only set-piece battle of Alexander's Indian campaign. His soldiers were becoming restless, and their morale and willingness to fight could no longer be taken for granted. In his efforts to appease local populations throughout the years of campaigning, Alexander had taken to adopting local dress and customs, to the intense disgust of the Macedonians, who felt that they were losing their pre-eminent place in his affections. Furthermore, they were a long way from home and, with Alexander driving ever more relentlessly onwards in search of new lands to conquer, it was some time since they had been allowed to relax and enjoy the spoils of victory. Their king had also grown intolerant of the huge baggage trains full of silver, gold, spices, jewellery, cloth and other riches which his army seemed to accumulate wherever it went, and which he felt impeded its progress, and several times had ordered it to be dispersed, to the dismay of all but his most dedicated troops. Too many now felt they had little or nothing to look forward to, and their mood was not improved by the fact that the previous two months of campaigning had been conducted during the monsoon season, and for most of the time they had been drenched to the skin. Foreseeing a campaign which involved much marching around and laying siege and skirmishing for scant reward, and disposed to take on trust rumours that the armies awaiting them to the east numbered hundreds of thousands of seasoned soldiers and scores of fearsome elephants, Alexander's army rebelled and refused point-blank to cross the river they thought was the Ganges (it was in fact the Hyphasis).

Alexander was mortified and retreated to his tent for three days, waiting for a change of heart. None came. A lengthy stand-off was averted when Alexander ordered sacrifices to be made and omens to be read: his diviners, who were not averse to a bit of well-judged diplomacy when the need arose, found these to be most unfavourable, and Alexander was able to order a change of plan without apparent loss of face. The army turned away from the east and, equipping themselves with a fleet of 800 river boats and galleys, set off downstream in search of what was known as the Southern Ocean, effectively leaving control of the lands to the east of the river in the hands of the defeated Prince Porus.

The king's response to this setback in the months which followed was to attempt to instil a new spirit of daring and adventure in his men by performing the most heroic feats of arms himself. Putting himself in charge of a lightly equipped force of Companion Cavalry, mounted archers, phalanx infantryman and light foot soldiers, Alexander led numerous raids on any local forces which attempted to resist or impede his passage south. The most warlike of these were the Malli tribe. After defeating them in open battle, Alexander pursued the remnants of the Malli force to their most heavily fortified city, where they had taken refuge. The outer walls of the town fell easily to the Macedonian infantry, but the attack faltered at the walls of the inner citadel. Seeing an opportunity to galvanize his men by his own example, Alexander sprang on to the first scaling ladder and led the assault on the battlements, but the weight of the men following behind snapped the ladder, leaving the king isolated on the battlements with only his shield-bearer Peucestas to protect him. But Alexander's blood was up. Disdaining to fight on the walls, the king leapt down into the citadel and stormed furiously into the throng of Malli soldiers below. Some reported seeing a dazzling sheet of flame rise up from the spot where he landed, others simply that he brandished his sword with such ferocity that none could get near him. However, after a few minutes of violent combat, Alexander's corselet was pierced by an arrow which penetrated his lung; simultaneously another of the Malli got behind him and struck him a heavy blow with a club to the back of the neck, and he collapsed at Peucestas's feet. The shield-bearer now took the brunt of the attack, protecting Alexander from further injury while the attacking force took advantage of the diversion to scale the walls unopposed and throw open the gates of the citadel.

Alexander was seriously injured. Outside the Malli town he underwent emergency surgery, losing blood at a rate which made his physicians fear for his life. Several days passed before it was considered safe to move him; then a small flotilla was assembled to bear him to his base camp. Shortly afterwards, to the anxious protestations of his physicians, Alexander got up off his bed and left his tent. He mounted his horse and rode slowly over to the encampment of a division of his Companion Cavalry. For a moment there was silence as his men observed the enfeebled but still upright figure of their king, his face pale from the pain and exhaustion. Then a shout went up:

'Hail Alexander! Hail Alexander the Great!'

The shout echoed across the camp. Then came a hoarse cheer from throats suddenly tight with emotion. The cheer echoed from camp to camp, and the outburst of rejoicing and relief reaching a crescendo as the entire army learned that their king, their hero, was safe.

The siege of the Malli town saw Alexander's last great act of heroism. Though he lived for another three years, leading his forces back towards their homeland by land, river and sea, the rigours of the campaigning life prevented him from making a full recovery from his injuries. Eventually his constitution proved inadequate to the task of fighting off a disease which struck him down while he was in Babylon in 323 BC, celebrating past triumphs with a prodigious round of drinking, and mustering another great army for a further campaign of glorious conquest.

The reception given to Alexander following his initial recovery from the wounds he received in the citadel indicates the strength of the bonds between him and his men. Almost as a matter of course, Alexander had placed his own life in severe jeopardy to save his forces from defeat – and every one of his soldiers knew that for an army of conquest far from home, defeat meant almost certain death. In numerous ways, Alexander had proved himself willing to share the hardships suffered by his soldiers, and though the demands he made of them were heavy, they were no heavier than the demands he made of himself. In this respect, Alexander was not just a king and a general, he was a soldier, too, who took his chances in battle just like any other.

Though he set himself up as a demi-god, the son of Zeus, and often acted in battle as if he thought himself immortal, Alexander was only flesh and blood and he knew it. When in great pain from the arrow wound received at the hands of the Malli, he remarked to his doctor: 'What you see flowing my friend, is blood.' As well as physical pain, Alexander must also have had to endure the doubts and anxieties which assail all men from time to time, but he concealed his sufferings for the sake of his men and his campaigns.

Alexander's was heroism on a grand scale, modelled on the exploits of the great heroes of the past and capable of inspiring a whole army of war-hardened soldiers to achieve the most improbable victories. The present era would perhaps be unsympathetic towards Alexander's motives –

in particular his ceaseless quest for conquest and self-glorfi-
cation – but in his day the achievement of battle honours
was considered an ambition of the highest moral worth.
That a mortal man should be capable of the heroic deeds
performed by Alexander the Great will always be a source
of wonder and admiration, for in terms of personal bravery
and willingness to sacrifice his life for his fellow soldiers,
the Macedonian conqueror may never be equalled.

Chapter Two

Horatio Nelson & the Battle of Cape St Vincent

I cannot, if I am in the field of glory, be kept out of sight: wherever there is anything to be done, there Providence is sure to direct my steps.

Horatio Nelson

On the night of 11 February 1797, a Royal Navy frigate, *La Minerve*, found herself in heavy fog in the Atlantic Ocean west of Gibraltar. The ship carried an important passenger. Sir Gilbert Elliot had been viceroy of Corsica, but the island had been abandoned by the British as untenable after the entry of Spain into the war against revolutionary France. The man assigned to bring Sir Gilbert home was Commodore Horatio Nelson.

Nelson, the son of a Norfolk rector, was thirty-eight years old, and had been at sea since he was twelve. He had become a lieutenant in the Royal Navy at the age of eighteen. He had fought a polar bear in the Arctic, the Spanish in Nicaragua, the American colonists, the French, had contracted malaria in Bombay, successfully besieged Bastia in Corsica and commanded a press gang in the ports of southern England. He had also spent eight years as a farmer in East Anglia. He had married the niece of the governor of a small British colony in the Caribbean. He was soon to fall in love with a blacksmith's daughter who also happened to be an ambassador's wife, Emma Hamilton.

At the beginning of 1797 Nelson's reputation was high with his peers, and his name was fearful to enemy captains. Eighteen months before he had proudly informed his wife that his ship, the *Agamemnon* (known to its crew as the 'egg and bacon'), 'is as well known through Europe as one of Mr Harwood's ships is at Overy'. But he was frustrated at the constant thwarting of his ambitions. In March 1795 he had fought French ships outside Toulon with considerable success, only to be ordered to disengage at exactly the moment he would have chosen to strike for comprehensive victory. He wrote to his wife: 'I wish to be an admiral and in command of the English fleet; I should very soon do much or be ruined. My disposition cannot bear tame and slow measures.'

At the beginning of 1796 things looked up. The slow-measured Admiral Hood was replaced as Commander-in-Chief of the British Mediterranean fleet by the more aggressive Sir John Jervis. Nelson knew, liked and admired Jervis, and the feeling was mutual. Jervis was quick to take Nelson into his confidence. The latter was told that he would be promoted soon to rear-admiral. For the meantime he was made a commodore, with an admiral's duties. In June 1796 he switched his pennant from the *Agamemnon* to the *Captain*, a seventy-four gun ship captained by the American-born Ralph Miller, and with which he was destined to make his name the following February. Jervis's appearance in the Mediterranean had done wonders for British morale, but in October Spain was impelled by Bonaparte's invasion of Italy to join the war on the French side. The British were in danger of being seriously outnumbered.

The British government decided that the situation was untenable. The Mediterranean was to be abandoned. Nelson organized the evacuation of Corsica and Elba. For the latter he shifted his Commodore's pennant to *La*

Horatio Nelson

Minerve. Shortly before picking up Sir Gilbert Elliot from Elba, *La Minerve* and the *Blanche* engaged two Spanish frigates and captured both before having to release them at the appearance of a sizeable Spanish squadron on the horizon.

From Elba *La Minerve* sailed for Gibraltar, where Nelson learned that the Spanish fleet had just passed into the Atlantic, having left Carthagena on 4 February. Nelson revictualled quickly, aware that this news was of grave importance.

If the Spanish fleet was heading north, then it was in order to join up with the French and Dutch fleets in Brest. Already an invasion of Ireland had been attempted, and had only been abandoned due to foul weather. Should the Spanish get through to Brest a new attempt would surely be made, with the most formidable protection. The war with revolutionary France had so far produced no great British victories. Morale in Great Britain was low, and dissent was flourishing. A victory was essential, both strategically and politically.

Nelson had done his own research into political dissent in his home county, and what was more he had recognized the justice of many of the complaints it thrived upon. However, he had no time whatsoever for sedition, be it on land or sea; he was a monarchist in every fibre of his body. He now had to decide whether the Spanish fleet was heading northwards or for the West Indies. He chose to believe the former, and therefore set to finding Jervis somewhere between Gibraltar and Cadiz.

As *La Minerve* left Gibraltar two Spanish line-of-battle ships, *Le Terrible* and *Bahama* both carrying seventy-four guns, came out of Algeciras in pursuit. Nelson told Captain George Cockburn to prepare for action, should the Spanish succeed in catching the British frigate. With that he sat down to dinner with the ex-Viceroy. Among those at table was First Lieutenant Thomas Hardy, who eight years later, as Captain of the *Victory*, was to bestow the most famous kiss in British history. No sooner had they started to eat than there was a cry of 'man overboard'.

Hardy was despatched with a longboat to try and find the man, but to no avail. The Spanish warships were gaining fast now, were almost within gunshot. Hardy turned to pull back to *La Minerve*. He could make no headway. Hardy had only recently escaped from Spanish captivity, and Nelson could not bear the thought of the young man being captured once more. 'By God! I'll not lose Hardy,' he declared, 'back the mizen topsail.' *La Minerve* turned and now faced the two Spanish battleships. It seemed as if an extremely unequal engagement was about to be fought.

Nelson's determination to pick up his friend had an unexpected effect on the pursuing Spanish. They must have assumed that Nelson had good reason to turn and fight, that a British fleet or squadron had appeared on the horizon, visible to the lookout of *La Minerve* but not to the Spanish. They backed their sails and returned to Algeciras. It was 11 February 1797. Nelson sailed on westwards. The fog descended.

Deep in that night Nelson made his way below deck to enquire of Colonel Drinkwater, the Viceroy's secretary, whether it would be appropriate to wake Sir Gilbert. There were two very large ships on either side of the frigate, well within hailing distance. Sir Gilbert awoke, and Nelson took him up to observe the 'strange ships'. The Commodore ordered his Captain to follow the movements of the large ships, and to make sure that silence was maintained amongst the crew. He knew it was not Jervis's fleet he was sailing with. He knew it was the Spanish.

By daybreak he had extricated himself from the Spanish without their having learned of the celebrated Nelson's presence among them. He spent the next day ascertaining that they were not heading westwards and on the lookout for Sir John Jervis and the British fleet. On the morning of the 13th, now sure that the Spanish were heading north, he found his compatriots and went straight to Jervis's flagship, the *Victory*.

Other sources confirmed Nelson's information and before sunset on the 13th Jervis gave the signal to prepare for battle. Ships were to stay in close order during the night. Nelson retuned to the *Captain*. At 2.30 a.m. a passing Portuguese frigate confirmed that the Spanish were close by.

The battle that was to come was to be fought between two fleets of very different strength. Sir John Jervis's fleet was severely under strength. Five ships-of-the-line (major warships) were currently being repaired, and until reinforcements arrived on 6 February he had been reduced to nine capital ships. Admiral Parker's arrival increased his strength to fifteen sail-of-the-line and four frigates. The Spanish fleet consisted of twenty-seven sail-of-the-line and ten frigates. What was more the Spanish ships were bigger. The Spanish admiral Don Jose de Cordoba was aboard the largest warship in the world, the *Serenissima Trinidad*. It had four decks and 136 guns. In addition he commanded six 112-gun ships. In contrast Jervis's flagship, the *Victory*, carried one hundred guns. Five further sail-of-the-line had over ninety guns apiece. On paper there should have been no question as to the outcome of any engagement. The British were outnumbered by two to one both in guns and ships.

Sir John Jervis was, however, a man of sanguine temper, and he was delighted with the officers under his command. He even went so far as to thank the Admiralty for the quality if not the quantity of his reinforcements – 'I thank you very much for sending me so good a batch. They are a valuable addition to my excellent stock.' Nelson echoed his Admiral's opinion: 'Of all the fleets I ever saw I never beheld one in point of officers and men equal to Sir John Jervis's, who is a commander-in-chief able to lead them to glory.'

Nelson's emphasis on 'men' as well as 'officers' was characteristic and well-founded. British gun crews could fire very much more quickly than their Spanish counterparts, in some estimates ten times faster. Most of the British seamen had been at sea far longer than the Spanish crews, and were consequently far more experienced. Most of them had taken part in a sea battle of some sort or another. Even while they loathed its cruelties they probably recognized the value of discipline once the cannon balls began to fly, and the musket shots ring out.

Perhaps most importantly the Spanish did not want to fight. Easterly winds had prevented them putting in to Cadiz, their actual destination. Nevertheless, Admiral Don Jose de Cordoba had little reason to be alarmed as he cruised off the Spanish coast, waiting for a change in the wind. After all, the British had only nine ships. He knew that because an American merchantman had told him so. On the night of the 13th the wind had indeed shifted, and the Spanish began to make their way, without much regard to order, towards land.

At daybreak on Monday, 14 February 1797 the British fleet was in good order, in two divisions. The morning was hazy and visibility far from perfect. There was very little wind. In short it was a perfect day for a battle at sea. At 6.30 a.m. *Culloden*, captained by Thomas Troubridge, a friend of Nelson's since their early teens, signalled that five ships had been spotted to the south-west. A little later *Niger* and *Lively* confirmed the sighting. The *Bonne Citoyenne* was sent to reconnoitre. The Spanish drew closer. 'By my soul, they are thumpers!' declared the signal lieutenant of the *Barfleur*, 'they loom like Beachy Head in a fog.' As more and more

Heroes

Spanish ships appeared over the course of the next two hours Sir Robert Calder, the Captain of the Fleet, reported to Sir John Jervis. These reports took on a feisty concision in subsequent tales of the battle that assured their immortality:

> *There are eight sail of the line, Sir John*
> *Very well, sir*
> *There are twenty sail of the line, Sir John*
> *Very well, sir*
> *There are twenty-seven sail of the line, Sir John; near double our own!*
> *Enough, sir! No more of that. The die is cast and if there are fifty sail of the line, I will go through them*

On the Spanish side there occurred a looseness of signalling that perfectly demonstrates the difference between the two fleets. The first Spanish ship had signalled the appearance of the British fleet, but no acknowledgement was made. The Captain then sent another signal, suggesting that the British were some forty strong. He afterwards claimed he had done this merely to rouse his admiral. In fact it perplexed him no end, and may have been responsible for the chaotic form his line of battle took.

At 8.15 a.m. Admiral Jervis put up the signal to form close order. At 9.30 the *Culloden*, the *Blenheim* and the *Prince George* were ordered to 'chace' the forward ships of the Spanish fleet. By 10.30 the entire enemy fleet was visible. At 11 a.m. Jervis ordered his ships to form line, and half an hour later communicated his intention to pass through the enemy line. In fact the enemy 'line' was something of a shambles, the fleet being split into two distinct groups. It was Jervis's intention to divide thoroughly the two divisions, thereby reducing the fighting size of the Spanish fleet from twenty-seven to eighteen.

John Keegan has written of sea warfare at this period:

[The Royal Navy's] raison d'être was victory . . . its admirals had usually pressed their attacks home. Yet they had not always, not indeed very often, decisively beaten the enemy. Why was that?

The answer is that . . . the potentially chaotic nature of sea warfare had resulted in over-organisation . . . as early as 1691 a set of fighting instructions had been issued which established 'line to line' as the preferred method of combat at sea . . . Admiral Byng was executed not because he had lost the battle of Minorca (1756) but because he had done so in breach of the permanent fighting instructions.*

Flouting the Fighting Instructions was clearly a risky business, but on those few occasions when it had happened comprehensive victories had been won. The most celebrated was Rodney's triumph against the French at the Battle of the Saints in 1782, although it was accidental, a prize of the elements. It was not until Trafalgar that the tactic of sailing through the enemy's line in two or more divisions, rather than fighting 'line to line', was recognized as being the most efficient use of the formidable fighting machines that these big warships represented. Initially Sir John Jervis's tactics at the Battle of Cape St Vincent were those of the Fighting Instructions. Had they been followed to the letter it is likely that the Spanish fleet would have regrouped or fled or (most likely) both.

The leading British ship was the *Culloden* . . . Spanish broadsides greeted her at about 11.30 a.m., but with little effect, and as the British ships followed her through the gap it was soon apparent that the Spanish had been effectively split. The small group of Spanish ships attempted to break

*John Keegan, *The Price of Admiralty* (London, 1988)

back through the British line, but were thoroughly repulsed by broadsides from the port sides of the British ships, and they disengaged, making off to the south-east.

At 12.08, the British now to the west of the Spanish, Jervis ordered his ships to tack in succession. This decision, although correct by the terms of the Fighting Instructions, meant that the British ships would straightforwardly follow the *Culloden* up the Spanish line. Better, or at least quicker, would have been to turn the line around, so that the ships at the end of the line, including the *Captain*, which was third from last, would become the van. The danger of Jervis's course was that it might give the two Spanish groups time to re-form. The Spanish admiral, seeing the British manoeuvre, steered east. It looked as if the Spanish might escape.

Nelson saw this at once and took decisive action. He 'hauled out' of the line and steered directly towards the head of the Spanish fleet. Colonel Drinkwater, watching with Sir Gilbert Elliot on *La Minerve*, which stood at a safe distance from the fighting, described Nelson's action as follows: 'His ship had no sooner passed the rear of the enemy's ships that were to windward, than he ordered her to wear and stood on the other tack towards the enemy. In exacting this bold and decisive manoeuvre, the Commodore reached the sixth ship from the enemy's rear, which was the Spanish admiral's own ship, the *Santissima Trinidad* of one hundred and thirty-six guns.'*

Nelson had flouted the Fighting Instructions without hesitation. Another great friend, Cuthbert Collingwood, commanding the *Excellent*, which was the last ship in the British line, followed at once. On board the *Victory* Sir Robert Calder asked Jervis if they should be recalled. 'No. I will not have them recalled. I put my faith in those ships. It

*Col. John Drinkwater, *A Narrative of the Battle of Cape St Vincent* (London, 1840)

is a disgrace they are not supported.' This suggests that Nelson knew his Admiral well enough to have taken the risk. Following the battle Calder brought up the question of Nelson's disobedience once more. The Admiral agreed: 'It was certainly so, and if ever you commit such a breach of your orders, I will forgive you also.'

Nelson had sailed into the heart of the Spanish fleet, and soon found himself doing battle, alone, with no less than seven Spanish ships-of-the-line, including the *Serenissima Trinidad*, the *San Josef*, the *Salvador del Mundo*, the *San Nicolas*, the *Mexicana* and the *San Ysidro*. He was fighting with seventy-four guns against some six hundred and fifty. *Culloden* arrived soon after, at about 1.30 p.m., and for an hour the two ships fought with the Spanish what Nelson described as an 'apparently, but not really, unequal contest'. At around 2.15 the *Blenheim* passed between them and the enemy ships. This gave the *Captain* a necessary respite, in which time her ammunition was replenished and some rigging repaired. The *Blenheim* loosed off a raking broadside, and the *Salvador del Mundo* and the *San Ysidro* fell back.

It availed them not at all. By now Collingwood had arrived in the *Excellent*, well-known as having the most devastating gunnery in the navy. The *Excellent* pulverised the two Spanish ships, and the *San Ysidro* struck its colours. It was about three o'clock. Nelson thought the *Salvador del Mundo* had also surrendered. 'But Collingwood,' he later reported, 'disdaining the parade of taking possession of beaten enemies, most gallantly pushed up, with every sail set, to save his old friend and messmate, who was, to appearance, in a critical situation.'

And indeed the *Captain* was taking a terrible pounding by some three or four big Spanish ships, one of which was the *San Nicolas*. She had lost her fore topmast, and most of her rigging. The wheel had been dashed to splinters. Furthermore, the *Culloden* and *Blenheim* had both retired, badly damaged. Collingwood steered for the *San Nicolas*, drew alongside, 'you could not put a bodkin between us', and loosed another thundering broadside which devastated the enemy ship and that abreast of it, the *San Josef*. The two Spanish ships became entwined by their wounds. Collingwood passed on to the *Serenissima Trinidad*, leaving Nelson to re-engage the ships he had already been battling for the last hour or two.

But the *Captain* was too badly damaged to continue as an efficient fighting ship. Nelson ordered a final broadside, which was responded to vigorously by the Spaniards, and then ordered Captain Miller to ram the *San Nicolas*. They were going to board her. The *Captain* smashed into the stern of the Spanish ship and the two were at once locked together in a mesh of masts and rigging. Still the *San Josef* could not extricate herself from the mêlée.

Once the marines of the 69th Regiment were across, Nelson followed, jumping from the fore chains of the *Captain* into the quarter-gallery of the *San Nicolas*. 'Two men left the ship with me, but one fell into the sea,' he reported afterwards. He found the cabin doors locked, and Spanish officers firing pistols through the internal windows. But the doors were soon smashed down, and Nelson pushed through to the quarterdeck. He arrived in time to receive the sword of the ship's dying commander.

From the poop deck and galleries of the *San Josef* next to the *San Nicolas*, Spanish muskets were 'sorely annoying' British troops on the deck of the *San Nicolas*. The question was whether to quit or whether to advance. There was never very much debating of such questions in the mind of Horatio Nelson. He led the boarding party onto the next ship. A Spanish officer, unarmed, appeared at the rail of the quarterdeck and said the ship had surrendered, and that the rear-admiral on board was dying below decks. Nelson insisted that the Spanish captain muster all his officers on

Nelson boarding the *San Jose* at the Battle of St Vincent, 1797

the quarterdeck. This was done. He asked them to surrender their swords. 'As I received them,' he later reported, 'I gave [them] to William Fearney, one of my bargemen, who placed them, with the greatest sang-froid, under his arm.' Nelson's eye for this kind of detail was absolutely characteristic. He was obviously delighted by it.

Shortly afterwards an ordinary seaman, long known to Nelson, approached the Commodore, excused himself of the liberty he was taking, and asked to shake him by the hand, congratulating him 'upon seeing me safe on the quarterdeck of a Spanish three-decker'. Nelson had boarded two ships at once, and no one had ever done that before.

There was not much time for celebration there and then, despite the *Victory* saluting the *Captain* as she sailed by, because there was now fire on board the *San Josef*. Nelson summoned firemen from the *Captain*, and the flames were doused before any great damage was done. It was 3.30 p.m.

At 4 p.m. the Spanish division that had been defeated in the morning re-appeared. The day was drawing on, the light beginning to fade. Jervis signalled a disengagement. Nelson left the stricken *Captain*, and returned to the *Minerve* which was eventually to tow the *Captain* home.

The Battle of Cape St Vincent was a major victory. British casualties were around 300 killed and wounded (some sixty of these on the *Captain* alone). The *Captain* was the only British ship to lose a mast. Four enemy ships were taken: the *San Nicolas* and the *San Josef* by Nelson, the *San Ysidro* by Collingwood and the *Salvador del Mundo* by Jervis himself. Losses on these ships alone were around 600. As for the *Santissima Trinidad*, that leviathan ship had escaped (though with 200 killed and wounded) much to the chagrin of Commodore Nelson. He was to come across her eight years later, at Trafalgar, where she was so badly damaged she sank in the huge gale which followed the battle. At Cape St Vincent 2,300 prisoners were captured.

The 'essential' victory was sensational. Nelson's feat in taking two major ships-of-the-line in one fell swoop electrified the nation. At the end of his own account of the battle Nelson appended the following: 'There is a saying in the fleet too flattering for me to omit telling – viz., "Nelson's Patent Bridge for Boarding First-rates", alluding to my passing over an Enemy's eighty-gun ship.' He added a joke which was doing the rounds of the fleet:

> *Commodore Nelson's Receipt for Making an Olla Podrida:*
> *'Take a Spanish first-mate and an eighty-gun ship and after well* **battering** *and* **basting** *them for an hour, keep throwing in your* **force-balls** *and be sure to let these be well* **seasoned**. *Your* **fire** *must never slacken for a moment, but must be kept up as brisk as possible during the whole time. So soon as you perceive your Spaniards to be well* **stewed** *and* **blended** *together, you must then throw your own ship on board the two-decker, back your spritsail yard to her mizzen mast, then skip in to her quarter-gallery window, sword in hand, and let the rest of your boarders follow as they can. The moment that you appear on the eighty-gun ship quarterdeck, the Spaniards will all throw down their arms and fly. You will then only have to take a hop, skip and jump from your stepping stone and you will find yourself in the middle of the first-rate quarterdeck with all the Dons at your feet.*
>
> *Your Olla Podrida many now be considered as completely dished and fit to be set before His Majesty.*
>
> *Nelson his art of cooking Spaniards.*

The Battle of Cape St Vincent severely diminished Spanish naval capability and thereby weakened the ability of the French to keep the British out of the Mediterranean.

Heroes

The following year, at the Battle of the Nile, Nelson destroyed the French fleet and secured British domination of the sea.

Sir John Jervis was made Earl of St Vincent, Nelson a Knight Commander of the Bath. His promotion to Rear-Admiral was confirmed immediately. He presented the Spanish rear-admiral's sword to the city of Norwich, of which town he was made a freeman. From Bath his father wrote to him: 'The name and services of Nelson have sounded throughout this city of Bath, from the common ballad-singer to the public theatre.' Nelson had become a star. He was to rise and rise. The victory at the Nile was followed by the destruction of the Danish fleet at Copenhagen in 1801. The last time he left England, in September 1805, he had to use back doors and secret routes to get to his ship, so huge were the crowds that gathered to see him off. To Captain Hardy he remarked, 'I had their huzzas before; I have their hearts now.' He died of his wounds on 21 October 1803, knowing he had won the greatest sea battle ever fought. He is certainly the greatest war hero in the history of Great Britain.

Chapter Three

Audie Murphy & the Battle of the Colmar Pocket

They can kill us, but they can't eat us. It's against the law.
Sergeant Lattie Tipton

In December 1944 Eisenhower's prediction that the Second World War would be over by Christmas looked decidedly off-beam. The Allies had stalled in their push for Berlin. Mainly it was a question of logistics. General Patton had been reduced to stealing large quantities of fuel from the US 2nd Army in order to propel his own force, the US 3rd Army. And it looked as though the winter was going to be hard.

Nevertheless High Command remained sanguine. It was simply a matter of time before the Germans surrendered. They were beaten.

On the foggy night of 16 December the Germans counterattacked with total surprise and breathtaking energy. Panzers punched through the Allied line where they had no business punching through the snow-fat forests of the Ardennes. The Americans were pushed back sixty miles. By Christmas Day the Germans were within four miles of the Meuse, almost ready to sweep north, take Antwerp and split the British and American Armies.

But now the Americans stopped retreating, and on 3 January the US 1st Army launched its counter-offensive. By

Heroes

28 January the Americans had regained all the ground that had been lost. The Battle of the Bulge had been won, at the cost of 80,000 American casualties.

The Battle of the Bulge 1944

On 16 December Hitler flung his last reserves of 250,000 men and 1,100 tanks into a desperate attempt to strike through the Ardennes and take the ports of Liège and Antwerp, in order to split the Allied forces in the north from those in France with the vain hope of then 'rolling-up' the front line. Though checked by the US 5th Corps in the north, the violence of the assault threw back the US 1st Army and 8th Corps. But after the Germans had reached Bastogne in the west on 20 December, they were halted in the south by the US 4th Infantry and 9th Armoured. Patton's 3rd Army then attacked the southern flank of the Germans' salient – the 'bulge' – and the German push to the west was halted in front of the Meuse by the British 29th Armoured and American 2nd Armoured. Bastogne was then retaken, and Allied bombers smashed the German convoys to cut off their supply lines. In January a concerted counter-attack pushed the Germans back and, having failed to retake Bastogne, they retreated. By the end of January they were back to their starting point, at a cost of 70,000 casualties, 50,000 prisoners, 600 tanks and 1,600 aircraft. The Allies lost 77,000 killed and wounded.

Two days before, far to the south, close to the intersection of France, Germany and Switzerland, where the Rhine turns east, an illiterate nineteen-year-old Irish Texan became the most decorated soldier in the history of the American Army. Audie Murphy was born in Texas on 20 June 1924, into a large family of tenant sharecroppers. They were very poor indeed. Murphy's father's alcoholism, gambling and absenteeism did not help. In 1933, at the height of the Depression, the family lived in a railroad boxcar, dependent entirely on relief. Murphy grew up on a diet of biscuits and gravy. Once he was old enough the family's diet was supplemented by what Murphy hunted. He became a very accurate shot: 'If I missed,' he said years later, 'we didn't eat.'

In November 1940 Murphy's father disappeared for good, and his mother fell ill. She was dead by the spring. He was sixteen years old.

On his eighteenth birthday, some six months after Pearl Harbor and the American entry into the war, Audie Murphy travelled to his local recruiting office. He was 5 foot 5 inches tall, and weighed about 8 stone. He was turned away on the grounds that he was too young. He returned a week later, with his birth certificate and a letter from his sister.

His fragile, childlike appearance was a source of constant irritation to him. Referred to by all as 'baby', commanders kept trying to give him soft options, in the cookhouse or with service platoons, and it took him some months to convince the army that he was proper soldier material.

Despite (or maybe because of) his coming from a large family, Audie Murphy was something of a loner. He was described by someone who had employed him (as a petrol pump attendant) before he went into the army as: 'honest, humble, shy, proud, and neat as a pin'. He also had a ferocious Irish temper. His hard upbringing gave

Audie Murphy

him a self-reliance which before long revealed itself to his military superiors. He was to be much appreciated. He wrote, years later, to his biographer, Charles Whiting: I have to admit, I love the damned army. It was father,

---

The Battle of the Atlantic 1940–1

The great four-year struggle to keep open Britain's supply routes from America, upon which it was utterly dependent. It cost the lives of 30,248 merchant seamen, and 51,578 Royal Naval personnel. By the summer of 1941, Britain and its Allies had lost over 1,200 ships, and imports had fallen by a third. It was the work of U-boats. Although the Allies sank thirty-one, the Germans soon had a hundred new submarines in the Atlantic. In 1942 U-boats sank 1,160 ships and almost brought Britain to its knees. But the introduction of 'Asdic' underwater detection, radar and new escort systems reduced losses and began to make inroads into the submarine fleet. Though the Germans had 250 U-boats operating in 1943, sixty-seven of them were sunk between March and May, and Admiral Doenitz was forced to recall them to rest and repair. By the time they returned to the attack, Allied merchant production was exceeding its decreasing losses. Morale was further raised when the Royal Navy sank the German battle cruiser *Scharnhorst*, which had ravaged merchant shipping. By the end of 1944 the battle was won, though the U-boat commanders struggled on until the end, then scuttled 221 of their surviving craft.

---

mother, brother to me for years. It made me somebody, gave me self-respect.'

In February 1943 Private (Acting Corporal) Murphy, boarded the *Hawaiian Skipper* to cross the Atlantic to Casablanca (as it happened *Casablanca* was the last movie he saw before leaving America). He was seasick all the way, but at least the voyage was free from the attentions of German U-boats.

Murphy was assigned to the 15th Infantry Regiment, one of the three regiments that made up the 3rd Infantry Division, but he was dismayed to find that he would now undergo yet further training. General Lucien Truscott, divisional commander, had studied the advanced training techniques of the British Army, in particular the 'battle school', and he now applied these to his raw soldiery. It proved, over the course of the war, to be necessary. The 3rd Infantry Division sustained more casualties – over 30,000 – than any other division. It also garnered no less than forty-six Medals of Honour (the highest award for valour in the American Army). This represented some one-fifth of all such decorations awarded during the entire war.

The division was a part of the US 7th Army, under the command of an erratic megalomaniac by the name of General Patton. The 7th Army invaded Sicily in July 1943, despite prodigious gales, which made Murphy among thousands of others horribly seasick.

During the invasion Murphy killed his first enemy soldiers (two Italians on white horses), was promoted to corporal, and wrote home: 'I have seen war as it actually is and I do not like it.' But he was also sick a good deal of the time; indeed he did not take part at all in Patton's superfluous siege of Messina.

Over the following two years Audie Murphy was in action virtually all the time, fighting with a division that was always to the fore. Of the 235 men of B Company who left Casablanca in July 1943, only two survived to 1945. One was Audie Murphy. This remarkable ability to survive must be put down to the sharpness of his instincts and reflexes (much attested to), a kind of numbed spirit born of the poverty of his childhood, and straightforward gambler's luck.

Once Sicily had been taken it was time to concentrate on Italy proper. Italy had surrendered on 8 September, and there was a false assumption amongst the Allies that all that was required was a kind of rolling-up operation which would take them to the Alps. Instead they found themselves up against one of the ablest Wehrmacht field marshals, Kesselring. They would be fighting Germans, not defeated Italians. Progress proved to be slow and bloody.

Winston Churchill himself intervened with a plan to speed up the campaign. The idea was to launch a seaborne invasion north of Kesselring's position, and thereby turn his flank. The seaside town selected for the attack was called Anzio.

It was taken with no opposition. Sergeant Murphy missed the initial action due to sickness. But the advantage of surprise was not pressed home. Too long was taken in consolidation of the position. Murphy rejoined his comrades in time to feel the force of a massive German counter-offensive led by the Luftwaffe. Eighteen thousand vehicles and 79,000 men confined in and around the small town of Anzio were like sitting ducks. The bombardment was ferocious.

Audie Murphy was assigned as Platoon Sergeant of B Company's 3rd platoon. He was in charge of forty men. He was nineteen years old.

That February 1944 found the Americans at Anzio constantly on the defensive. Apart from the constant shelling, there were other problems, not the least of which was trenchfoot. Murphy 'neat as a pin' washed his socks and feet constantly. He insisted his men do likewise. He was fierce in his loyalty to them. He took care of them. In March he provided more conventional evidence of his qualities of leadership by single-handedly disabling a German tank.

He then promptly fell ill again.

In May 1944 the Americans were prepared to break out from Anzio. This they did with spectacular success, only to find themselves directed towards yet another superfluous target by yet another vain American general, Mark Clark.

General Clark wanted to be the liberator of Rome, though the eternal city was of no real strategic importance. His moment of glory was paid for by 50,000 casualties and the contempt of history.

But by August 1944 the war in Italy was indeed almost over, and the Allies turned their minds towards southern France. The idea was to land troops in the south, march north and link up with the Normandy armies.

Audie Murphy landed with the first wave of the 15th Infantry Regiment. The fighting was desultory, the German 19th Army retreating in as good order as it could. But Murphy did see action, and the death of his best friend, Lattie Tipton. Before an action Tipton would always remark that 'they can kill us, but they can't eat us. It's against the law.' In Provence that summer Murphy's platoon appeared to have defeated a number of Germans on a hill feature. The Germans had waved a white flag to indicate surrender and Tipton, against Murphy's urgings, had risen to accept. He was mown down in a burst of machine-gun fire, and fell back into his friend's arms.

Enraged, and made fearless by his anger, Audie Murphy charged the German machine-gun nest, killing two Germans, wounding two more and forcing the rest to surrender. For this action he was awarded the Distinguished Service Cross. After the war he presented it to his friend's daughter.

The German 19th Army withdrew in good order, and the Americans made a somewhat bucolic advance through France. In September the action shifted eastwards. The Germans had taken up positions in the Vosges mountains, which overlooked the Rhine plain to the east. Here Audie Murphy was wounded for the first time, by shrapnel from a mortar.

The Battle of Arnhem 1944

After breaking out from Normandy, Montgomery put forward an ambitious plan to outflank German defences by securing bridges across the Maas, Waal and Lower Rhine. In operation Market Garden, on 17 September, three airbornes divisions – the US 101st and 82nd and the British 1st – were parachuted in between Nijmegen and Arnhem. The Americans took and held bridges over the Maas and Waal, but the British landed too far from the bridge at Arnhem to seize it with ease. They fought their way to Arnhem but were then attacked by the 9th SS Panzer, whom they repulsed in bitter fighting – so violent that the Germans were ultimately reluctant to engage them. As they held out against infinitely greater forces, an attempt by the Polish Parachute Brigade to relieve them failed, and on 25 September some 2,400 survivors withdrew by boat. The rest were finally compelled to surrender. They lost 1,130 dead; 6,450 were taken prisoner. German casualties were over 3,000.

He was back in time to win a Silver Star and the Legion of Merit for single-handedly taking out a German machine-gun nest which happened to be pinning down a group of the battalion's senior officers. For good measure he won a second Silver Star four days later, again around the Cleurie Quarry.

In October 1944, very much against his own wishes, Murphy was made an officer. Indeed he actually had to be ordered to accept the promotion. The US Army was having to promote on battlefield merit, so short had it become of officers. When Murphy and several others became officers they had to be discharged as enlisted men, and freshly commissioned as officers. 'You are now Gentlemen by act of Congress,' their commanding officer told them. 'Shave, take a bath and get the hell back into the lines.'

The weather that autumn was wet, very wet, and as the 3rd Infantry Division advanced higher into the Vosges the rain became frost and then snow. Progress was slow. There seemed to be a German sniper in every tree. On 25 October Murphy was hit by one. He was in hospital for two months. Still he was not sent home.

By the time Audie Murphy got back to the front the Battle of the Bulge was on. Troops had been moved north to counter the German attack, and the 7th Army, including the 3rd Infantry Division, was left to defend a huge front that stretched from Saarbrücken in the north to Switzerland in the south, some ninety miles.

By 28 December the Americans had turned the tide in the north, but the Germans had one last card left to play. Operation Northwind.

Shortly after the war Colonel Linger of the 17th SS Panzer Grenadier Division told investigators that 'When the break-through in the Ardennes had been stopped by the Allies, it was realized that several American divisions had been sent north to aid the Americans in their defence. It was therefore decided to launch an attack against what we felt sure to be a weak position.'

It was unlikely that Northwind would have changed the course of the war, but it had real aims: the recapture of Strasbourg; the defeat of the US 7th Army and the consequent halt of the American counter-attack in the Ardennes; the taking of Alsace-Lorraine might result in the fall of de Gaulle's goverement, with the likelihood of a communist seizure of power; communications and supply lines from the USA and the UK across France would be severely confused; perhaps the Allied coalition would collapse.

The German attack would be two-pronged. German Army Group B would break through in the north and drive south while the German 19th Army would break out of their forward position in the south, known as 'the Colmar Pocket' and head north. The Allied Army would be caught between the two.

Operation Northwind was launched at midnight on 31 December 1944. It failed. Although the Germans made some progress in all sectors, the French and Americans held. The Colmar Pocket bulged to the Vosges, but soon the tide was turned. The Americans began to regain lost ground. By the middle of January the Germans in the north had been repulsed, but the Allies did not have the strength to go on the counter-attack. In the south the Colmar Pocket turned into a hard malevolent cyst, which continued to be a danger to the American right flank. It had to be operated on. The Battle of the Colmar Pocket began on 22 January.

The Fecht River is a tributary to the Ill. The Ill in turn joins the Rhine sixty miles to the north, at Strasbourg. Just south of the conjoining of the Fecht and the Ill is the town of Colmar, famous for Grünewald's Issenheim altar piece, a fifteenth-century series of religious paintings of ferocious intensity, and featuring a nightmare vision of the crucifixion, a portrait of Christ the man, his suffering awful.

Heroes

It was for this town, at the centre of the 'Colmar Pocket', that the Americans and Germans fought for sixteen days in January and February 1945. And it was just to the north, near the hamlet of Holtzwihr, that Audie Murphy mounted a one-man stand against six Panzers and 500 German infantry, and won.

The Allied plan for lancing the Colmar Pocket was straightforward. They would cross the Ill and head south, cutting the German line of retreat, and then either move west on Colmar itself or east to Neuf-Brisach on the Rhine. What was not so straightforward was the weather. The winter was the coldest in living memory. The temperature stayed at 20 degrees below zero and the snow was hip-deep in places. Tank engines seized up, artillery lenses became useless, and men had to find shelter in the flat, grey, frozen plain of the Rhine. Frostbite and pneumonia were as lethal enemies as German sharpshooters and Tiger tanks.

The 3rd Infantry Division, along with the 1st French Motorised Infantry, would lead the attack. The 30th, 7th and 254th Infantry Regiments crossed the Fecht on the night of 22 January and headed for the Ill. By dawn the division was dug in on the west bank of the larger river, and during the day elements of the 30th moved across an old stone bridge. Progress was good until about midday, when it became clear that German tanks, Tigers, had begun to make their presence felt. Armoured support was necessary, but the first attempt to get Shermans on to the east bank of the Ill was disastrous. The bridge collapsed. The 30th was now more or less stranded. One by one its battalions began to withdraw, under ferocious attack from the elite German forces of the 2nd Mountain Division. The Americans could find no cover in the unforgiving landscape. They lost radio contact with their supporting infantry. Their bazookas were useless against the heavy armour of the Tigers. By nightfall the 2nd Battalion had lost 350 men, half its fighting strength. The regiment had retreated in confusion back across the Ill.

But the bridgehead must be established, and now the divisional commander, General 'Iron Mike' O'Daniel, ordered the 15th Infantry Regiment into the battle. At dawn on the 24th, a new bridge now erected by engineers, they crossed the Ill with two Shermans and a tank destroyer. The 3rd Battalion made some headway but was again pushed back to the river. The 2nd Battalion was thrown in. The following day, the 25th, the Germans counter-attacked in force, and the 2nd Battalion too was repulsed. The 1st Battalion had got as far as the outskirts of the two villages, Holtzwihr and Riedwihr, which had to be taken before the bridgehead could be regarded as secure.

On the night of the 24th Audie Murphy and his comrades in B Company had tried to get some rest in the woods north-west of the two villages. It had been a freezing, grim few hours. At one point Murphy, almost asleep, had raised his head at the sound of a nearby cannon. As he did so he felt a pain in his head. His hair had frozen to the ice, and large clumps of it remained stuck to the earth.

The following day they moved closer to Riedwihr, but found the German defence becoming more vigorous. Murphy was hit in the leg by splinters from a mortar. This added to the limp he carried from his previous wound in the autumn.

During that day the 1st Battalion of the 15th penetrated 600 yards, but they were low on ammunition. They were also low on men. B Company had gone into action with 155 men and six officers. By the evening of the 25th twenty-eight men were commanded by two officers. The battalion as a whole disengaged and tried, as best it could, to dig in. In fact such a thing was impossible, the ground being far too hard.

At 1 a.m. orders came for Murphy's B Company to change direction, and head due south for Holtzwihr, to the west of

Riedwihr. There they should dig in, and wait for fresh troops to pass through them on the way to attack Riedwihr.

They reached the edge of the woods facing Holtzwihr at around 3 a.m. Again it was pointless trying to dig. Nonetheless, Murphy ordered his men to try, if only to keep themselves warm. Otherwise they should jog.

B Company's position was at the 'butt end' of a U of woodland, the sides of which stretched down towards Holtzwihr. A narrow road, running through the forest to the village, made the central line of the triton. A drainage ditch ran along its right-hand side. Come dawn B Company would see the steeple of the church and the housetops about a mile away, across open fields.

During the morning Murphy's men were joined by two tank destroyers.

Murphy called in to ask for orders. No troops had come through them, nor, with the exception of the tank destroyers, had they had any reinforcements. The orders were to hold.

Shortly after lunch Murphy became convinced that the Germans were preparing to attack. German tanks were warming up. A mortar barrage started. Six Tiger tanks could now be seen distinctly at the edge of the village, where they split into two groups of three, and began to manoeuvre towards the woody tines.

At this development one of the two American tank destroyers promptly drove straight into the drainage ditch. The machine-gun squad was hit by a mortar. The second tank destroyer received a direct hit.

German troops, deadly specks dressed in their white 'spook suits', could now be seen advancing through the snow. Murphy called up covering fire from his artillery, but it did not deter the Germans. They kept coming. Soon the Tigers' machine-guns were raking US lines. Murphy ordered his depleted company to pull back.

His company, indeed, but not Murphy himself. He was going to remain with the field telephone, directing artillery as best he could onto the advancing Germans. But these Germans were now within 200 yards. Murphy kept firing his carbine until he ran out of ammunition. He turned to run, but then noticed the burning tank destroyer. There on its turret was a perfectly good machine-gun, and several cases of ammunition.

In order to install himself Murphy had to drag the heavy telephone to the top of the turret and turf out the dead lieutenant. On the open line of the phone Murphy was being asked how close the enemy was: 'Hold the phone close and you can talk to the bastards.'

To the rear his men watched as Murphy prepared to take on the ludicrous odds. 'Kraut tanks rumbled past Murphy's position, passing within fifty yards of him and firing as they went by. They did not want to close in for the kill because they wanted to give our tank destroyer, which was burning, but not in flames, as wide a berth as possible,' said Lieutenant Walter Weispfennig, a forward artillery observer whose radio had not worked, thereby requiring the use of the field telephone to accurately plot supporting artillery fire.

Murphy was now totally exposed, except that the Germans could not quite credit where his fire was coming from. In the cold grey light of late afternoon the German infantry, perhaps 250 strong, confused themselves and took casualties. The Tigers, however, had started firing at the abandoned tank destroyer. Meanwhile German artillery pounded the area mercilessly. The open telephone line caught everything. 'Are you still alive, Lieutenant?' asked a sergeant at the other end, somewhat illogically. 'For the moment, yeah. And what are *your* post-war plans?' asked back Murphy.

To Murphy's right there was a snow-filled gully which

gave German infantry the kind of cover they needed to approach the crazy Irishman. A dozen infantrymen tried. Murphy, instincts and reflexes as one, cat-like, turned and pumped his .50 calibre machine-gun into them. On his other side Germans had got to within ten yards. Bullets ricocheted off the tank destroyer. Still it smouldered, ready to go off at any moment. Still Murphy held his ground, though he knew he could not hold much longer. He called up an artillery barrage, directing it onto his own position, and then the phone went dead.

The next thing that happened was one of those lucky moments which attach to great soldiers. The Germans ceased firing, the clouds parted, the sun shone for about twenty minutes and American dive-bombers attacked. The Germans began to withdraw.

Audie Murphy lowered himself down from the turret of the tank destroyer. His raincoat was full of holes; the map he had been holding in his left hand to aid the artillery was in tatters. The tank destroyer was riddled. He felt a dull pain in his leg, and looked down. His trouser leg was heavy with blood. Murphy limped back into the woods along the road, not once looking back. This was not bravado but exhaustion. He had killed or wounded an estimated thirty-five Germans in the one hour of the engagement.

The following day the 3rd Battalion took Holtzwihr with ease because the Germans had begun to withdraw from the Colmar Pocket, and were pulling back to the Rhine. Soon they would spend their last night in France.

The ancient fortifications of Neuf-Brisach were un-manned when the Americans moved in on 10 February. Now all that stood between them and Germany was the Rhine. The 15th Regiment went into reserve, Audie Murphy went to Paris. From there he was summoned to Nancy on 5 March, where he was awarded two Silver Stars and the Distinguished Service Cross. He was informed at the same time that he had won the Medal of Honour, the highest award for valour in the US Army, for his action at Holtzwihr. It was pinned on him on 2 June, along with the Legion of Merit. A week later he left Europe.

He returned home a star. The army treated him with kid gloves, removing him from active service while in Europe, and surrounding him with PR people for his reappearance in America. In due course he became a movie star, thanks in no small degree to the efforts of Jimmy Cagney. But with the exception perhaps of *The Red Badge of Courage*, a film version of Stephen Crane's great novel about cowardice and courage in war, he made no classics. He never pretended otherwise – 'the same film over and over again, for twenty-five years,' he once complained. In 1968 he went bankrupt, and in 1970 was charged with intent to commit murder – of a dog trainer who had mistreated a friend's pet. He was acquitted. He died in 1971, in a plane crash. He was buried with full pomp and ceremony in Arlington cemetery. The Vietnam war was not quite over, and that was a war from which no heroes emerged, no matter how brave certain individuals proved themselves to be.

Audie Murphy was a reluctant hero, 'a fugitive from the law of averages' as he once put it, but he was a hero nonetheless. He was not simply lucky. After his death Bill Maudlin, a cartoonist and actor, who had appeared with Murphy in *The Red Badge of Courage*, wrote in *Life* magazine: 'Every time he got into trouble . . . great numbers of people rallied to his help. This was not because he had won those medals. It was because most of us accept a certain amount of blending as we go along . . . Not Murphy. In him we all recognized the straight raw stuff, uncut and fiery as the day it left the still.'

Chapter Four

Douglas Bader

Sir Winston Churchill was always an eloquent man, but for the fighter pilots who defended Britain from the bombing raids of the Luftwaffe in 1940 he reserved one of his most powerfully moving pronouncements: 'Never in the field of human conflict has so much been owed by so many to so few.'

This short sentence of praise has a special place in the memories of all who lived through the blitz, and remains deeply resonant of the heroic sacrifices made during the darkest days of the Second World War. But of all those who fought in the skies over Britain, hurling their battered Spitfires and Hurricanes at wave after wave of German Junkers and Messerschmitts, one man seems to symbolize the indomitable defiance, the bulldog spirit of unquestioning bravery in the teeth of overwhelming odds, that inspired Churchill's most famous utterance. That man was Douglas Bader.

Even as a child, Douglas Bader seemed destined to play a brilliant role in whatever field of endeavour he chose, although his immediate family never treated him as if he were specially gifted. His mother, Jessie Amos, was a beautiful and spirited woman, if somewhat headstrong and tempestuous; his father, twenty years her senior, was a gruff, strong-willed man whom Jessie's charms had tempted out of apparently confirmed bachelorhood. Frederick Bader was an engineer in the army, and his skills were as much in demand after the end of the First World

War as during it, so the two boys saw little of him; and when he died from the after-effects of a shrapnel wound, it was difficult for them to feel much of a sense of loss. Douglas had an older brother, Frederick junior, who was his mother's favourite, and at times it seemed as if Douglas would have to fight for everything in life that his brother took for granted. But everyone agreed that Douglas was a remarkably spirited lad who took life much as he found it, and certainly wasn't one to bear a grudge.

After Frederick senior's death, Jessie married a Yorkshire vicar whose home was a cold rambling vicarage which the boys didn't much like, but their stepfather was a kindly man and the family was happy enough.

It was at school that Douglas began to show exceptional abilities. He was a bright, if somewhat idle pupil, but on the games field he was in a class of his own. He had a naturally quick eye and was superbly well balanced and athletic; this, combined with his eager, confident temperament, made him a natural for most sports. At cricket he was a swashbuckling batsman who scored mostly in fours and sixes, peppering the boundary even when the quality of the bowling deserved respect. Though probably too impatient to make the very top rank, he stood out from his peers throughout his schooldays, and would later play for the Combined Services against touring Test sides. He was even better at rugby. Douglas had plenty of speed and flair, but also relished the hard physical contact the game demands. He played at fly-half, and at the age of fifteen was good enough to be playing in the first XV with boys three years his senior. Always in the thick of the action, he was the sort of player who seemed impossible to catch when he had the ball – and when he was tackled, he seemed to bounce back off the pitch as if made of rubber. Shortly after he left school, Bader was picked to play for the Harlequins club, and it seemed that it was only a matter of time before he took his place in the England team.

Squadron Leader Douglas Bader on the wing of his Hurricane

Heroes

Douglas was popular, too. His tremendous vitality and sense of adventure meant that he was always the first to accept a dare, and could be relied upon to find some new and exciting outlet for boyish energies and enthusiasms. Those who knew him remembered that he always seemed thoroughly immersed in life, never holding himself back or keeping anything in reserve. His teachers responded to his openness – the fact that you always knew where you were with Douglas, even if where you were happened to be punishing a particularly rumbustuous boy for his latest act of derring-do. Though some considered that his determination all too soon shaded into obstinacy and that his self-confidence sometimes amounted to arrogance, others detected that beneath the ready-for-anything, freestyle attitude to life lay an intelligence and sensitivity that would stand him in good stead if he was ever called upon to do more than puff out his chest and pile in. Certainly it was no good trying to force Douglas to do anything . . . But if you appealed to his innate good sense and decency – and, as he matured, to his ambitions, then he was usually ready to listen. At any rate, one master at St Edward's, the school Douglas attended between the ages of thirteen and eighteen, had so much respect for him that he secretly paid Douglas's school fees for him when his mother and step-father could no longer afford them.

One of Douglas's aunts married a pilot who had served in the early days of the Air Corps and was now adjutant of the Royal Air Force College at Cranwell. Cyril Burge never directly encouraged Douglas to think of flying, but when the young lad came to stay he would spend hours in the garden watching the Avro 504 training aircraft rumbling overhead as the cadets practised their manoeuvres. When the kindly Cyril lifted the boy into the cockpit of an Avro, Douglas was instantly hooked: sitting excitedly in the confined space, bristling with instruments and controls which held the key to the miracle of flight, his imagination was fired by the thought that one day he might take these controls in his hands and steer the aircraft up, up into the wide open spaces of the sky.

Not many years later, Douglas was back at Cranwell as Flight Cadet Bader, learning to fly Avros under the skilled, patient tutelage of Flying Officer Pearson. A short, chunky man who never showed off to his pupils like some instructors but piloted his craft with immaculate artistry, Pearson taught Bader not to force but to coax the Avro into doing what he wanted, and helped him to develop that feel for the capabilities of an aeroplane which only many hours of flying can bring.

If Pearson was generally undemonstrative, Bader and his fellow cadets were not. They delighted in aerobatics, and vied with each other to perform the most outrageous stunts. The Avros had two cockpits – one for the instructor at the front, one for the cadet behind – and one favourite antic on a solo flight involved climbing from the rear cockpit, straddling the fuselage of the aircraft and gripping with the heels, then tying a handkerchief round the joystick of the front cockpit before returning to the rear. Of course it was a dangerous and foolhardy activity, but to the cadets the main risk was of being found out. Several times Bader's over-exuberant flying got him into trouble with his superiors; but he was clearly an immensely gifted pilot, and given his vital, outgoing nature it seemed churlish, somehow, to curb his zest for his new-found skill.

After Cranwell, Bader moved on to Kenley, home of 23 Squadron which flew Gloster Gamecock fighters. This tough, stubby little aircraft was the most acrobatic machine in the RAF, and Douglas honed his flying skills until he could tumble around in the skies with the best of them. All the cadets were aiming to be chosen to perform the flying display at Hendon, but with Commander Harry Day in the first plane, only one other place was available: Bader was chosen, and he and Day put on a faultless and exhilarating display. Not long afterwards, the South African rugby side, the Springboks, arrived in England for a Test match tour. It was clear that Bader had a chance to be picked for the England team and, playing fly-half for the Combined Services against the Boks in front of the England selectors, Bader performed valiantly, covering every inch of the field and taking on the huge Afrikaner forwards with gusto, despite breaking his nose shortly before half-time.

At the age of twenty-one, everything seemed to be going right for him. He had conquered his aversion for mathematics and passed his final exams to become Flying Officer Bader, a man who plainly had a brilliant career in the RAF ahead of him. Ruggedly handsome and always so thoroughly and happily engaged with whatever life had to offer him, Bader was exciting the attention of several young women who attended parties at Kenley. One or two of his superiors had misgivings – Bader sometimes seemed too high-spirited for his own good – but his guileless charm and passion for flying were infectious and undoubtedly contributed to the morale of his colleagues. Given more responsibility, it seemed likely that he would grow out of his tendency to leap first and look later.

23 Squadron took delivery of the last word in fighter planes, the Bristol Bulldog. Though considerably faster and more powerful than the Gamecock, the Bulldog was also heavier and less agile. The more dangerous aerobatic manoeuvres – slow rolls at low altitude being a prime example – were markedly more hazardous in an aircraft that tended to lose height quickly and could not so readily be brought out of a roll or dive. Commander Day did not exactly embargo low-level aerobatics – he knew that the best pilots were and always would be individualists who

could rise to the challenge of taking full charge of an aircraft in a dogfight, and that they had to know for themselves where the absolute limits of their capabilities lay – but he warned his pilots to be absolutely sure of what they were doing.

In December 1931, Bader and two colleagues dropped in on Woodley airfield. They met some tyro pilots who asked Bader, the hero of the Hendon display, some questions about aerobatics, then suggested he gave a demonstration by 'beating up' the airfield – an RAF term for a series of dramatic low-level stunts. At first Bader, mindful of Day's cautions about showing off, refused. One of the young men goaded him about being 'windy'. When he climbed into his aircraft, Bader was tight-lipped with fury. After gaining height, he banked steeply and swooped back down towards the airfield, the Bulldog's engine thundering, the hefty plane bucketing slightly in the thermals. Coming in low over the grass, the Bulldog's nose lifted slightly and she began a slow roll to the right. The throttle was well back, to keep the engine running, when Bader felt her drop. He thrust the stick hard over – the wings were vertical now. She was coming out of the roll, just through the most dangerous point but still losing height, when the left wingtip caught the grass and sent the Bulldog catapulting nose-first into the ground.

One minute, all grace and power; the next, a broken mess hissing quietly, flagged by a plume of hot dust.

And a young pilot, dazed and bleeding in a cage of tortured steel.

Bader was eased gently from the cockpit and stretched out on the airfield. A steward dashed up with a brandy on a tray. Bader told him calmly that he didn't drink A young Australian pilot administered first aid. Bader punched him on the chin for his pains – though the blow was a feeble one. He drifted in and out of consciousness as he waited for the

ambulance to arrive, losing blood fast, his body traumatized into numbness by the shock of the accident. All the
medical personnel who witnessed his injuries in those first
hours after the accident were in little doubt that Bader was
going to die.

At hospital they could do little but make the patient
comfortable and wait. He was far too weak to survive an
anaesthetic, and his pulse kept weakening to the point
where death seemed inevitable. Yet somehow he would
pull through, and as the hours wore on the bouts of
weakness lessened and the patient grew stronger. The
surgeon, knowing the dangers of infection in either of his
mutilated legs, was anxious to operate, and eventually it
seemed worth the risk: Bader would probably not survive
the operation . . . but he would certainly die without it. On
the operating table, there was just time to amputate the
right leg above the knee and clean up the left before Bader
began to sink again. Post-operative shock was now
draining him of resistance: he was nearly without a pulse,
and cold to the touch.

And yet he would not die . . . The next morning he
seemed to be stronger again, and the surgeon came round
to check on the state of his legs. The stump of his right leg
seemed to be OK, but the doctor's heart sank when he saw
the left: it was swollen and puffy, and giving off the sickly
odour that signals the onset of gangrene. The leg would
have to come off – and soon. Later that day, Bader was back
on the operating table, fighting again for his life as his body
endured once more the underhand, insidious blow of a
powerful dose of anaesthetic combined with the trauma of
the surgeon's steel.

Bader woke to pain – constant, obsessive pain which
would not leave him but nagged and cut away at his
resolve. His pallor went grey, his eyes sank deep into their
sockets, his body alternately writhed and stiffened as the

waves of agony gathered again and again washed over him. It was his absent left leg that was hurting him, the torn and shredded nerves screaming in outrage. He could not sleep for the pain, nor stay awake and alert enough to distract himself from it. For the third time since the crash, it seemed inevitable that Bader would die.

He remembered waking and finding the pain gone. Through a window opposite he could see a patch of sky. He felt an overwhelming sense of peace and clarity. Nothing much mattered. He could just lie back and relax. Forget about it all.

Then he heard a voice, a woman's voice, scolding: *Sssh! Don't make so much noise. There's a boy dying in there.*

The words seemed to pierce through the peace and clarity. So that was what was happening! Bader decided he was not going to die. He stopped relaxing, and almost by conscious act of will re-assembled the dissipating parts of his tortured body, called them together, welcomed back the pain . . . For a while he was wide awake, then delayed shock took effect and he fell into a state of unconsciousness from which he did not emerge for two days. Once he sat bolt upright in bed, kissed the nurse who was tending him, then fell back into coma. Even when he finally came round, there were a further two days of drifting in and out of consciousness before his doctors really felt that they could say that he was out of immediate danger.

But the battle was far from over. Bader was determined that he would learn to walk again, without crutches, even though there was no known example of anyone with two false legs having done so before. The process of learning to master the clumsy metal legs threatened to drain him of his hard-won vitality once more: there were the endless fitting sessions, as the specialists devised ways of holding his new legs securely in position; the torture of the straps that chafed raw patches round his upper thighs, and the awful claustrophobic feeling of being cramped and straitjacketed by the straps that went up over his shoulders; the violence and indignity of his early attempts to walk unaided which, for day after day after day, ended only with Bader on the floor, legs splayed out, bruised and exhausted in spirit as much as in body.

Those around him, including his new girlfriend, Thelma, whom he had encountered at a tearoom on one of his first outings from the hospital, learned to keep their distance when Douglas was learning to walk: his pride would neither allow him to rest for one minute until he had mastered the unwieldy contraptions which carried him, nor would it accept the hand outstretched to help him when he fell. This was the difficult, less attractive side of Bader's immense spirit: and yet without it, who can say whether he would have ever have walked again, let alone gone on to achieve things which would have been worthy of the utmost admiration even in an able-bodied man.

Slowly, the little triumphs began to happen more frequently, and the setbacks and disappointments less often. He could walk, for the most part, without falling, his extraordinary sense of balance and natural strength keeping him upright against all the odds. He found that he could even manage to dance, though in rather ungainly fashion. He could drive his car (and have accidents in it, as he soon discovered). He could play a passable game of doubles tennis, if his partner did most of the running, and his eye was good enough to let him play an innings of cricket – since he had always been inclined to score in boundaries, his lack of speed between the wickets was not much of a drawback.

But more than anything else, Bader longed to see if he could fly again. His success with his car was reassuring, since a car required far more legwork than a plane would do. Then

Bader was not averse to getting some fun out of his disability. Occasionally, he would come across someone who complained of a stiff knee or a twisted ankle. 'Have it off, old boy, have it off!' was his immediate response, as he picked up his right leg and waved it encouragingly at the startled sufferer.

While staying with friends during his convalescence, Bader came into conflict with the resident terrier, a testy character with very fixed ideas about the order of things in its household. One evening at dinner, Bader's foot got a little too close to the spot under the table where the terrier was accustomed to lie at mealtimes, and a warning growl was heard. Bader moved his foot temptingly close. There was a louder growl, then the sound of teeth snapping into metal . . . then a yelp of surprise and the terrier shot out from underneath the table with its tail between its legs and the laughter of the assembled guests ringing in its ears.

he was invited to stay for the weekend with the Under-Secretary of State for Air, Sir Philip Sassoon, who lived on the edge of the Lympne airfield where 601 Squadron came to practise in summer. Sassoon mentioned that there was an Avro 504 there, and wondered whether Bader would like a crack at it. Bader needed no second bidding. and the next morning he was airborne again.

To his delight, he found that all his old skills came back to him – his feeling for the air, his confident but delicate movements of stick and rudder, his easy absorption in the complex business of aircraft handling which it is given to some to achieve as if they were born to it. He took off, circled and landed a few times, and each manoeuvre was sweeter to him than the last.

He knew there were a number of processes to be endured before he would be allowed to fly solo again: he had to be assessed both by RAF doctors and by the Central Flying School at Wittering, but surely these would be mere formalities now. At Wittering his instructors soon decided there was nothing they could usefully teach him. Now Bader longed to fly solo again. He knew he could not do so until passed fit for flying, and it was with a surge of anticipatory happiness that he received the summons to go to London for a formal assessment. It seemed certain that he would be back on flying duties within the month.

Which made the downpouring of misery even worse when the wing commander told him that there was nothing in the King's Regulations which covered his case, and that he could not therefore be passed fit for flying.

Many would have given way to bitterness at such a blow. After all he had been through, all he had worked for, all he had achieved . . . to be stymied not even by a regulation, but by the lack of a regulation – that seemed cruel indeed. Instead of flying, Bader devoted himself to Thelma, the love of his life, whom he married shortly after leaving the RAF. Short of money, stuck in a routine office job that seemed like an insult to his ebullient character, it was Thelma who kept his spirits up in these difficult times. Facing the challenge of civilian life was a sobering experience for the young airman, suddenly deprived of the clubbable comradeship of the RAF, who had never before had to worry about where to lay his head at night and how to pay the rent. In many ways, the end of Bader's convalescent

---

SBS: Mediterranean Raiders

Formed in 1941 as an irregular hit-and-run force, the British Special Boat Squadron (SBS) had an almost unrivalled élan. This was perfectly captured in an incident where a junior SBS officer, Andy Clark, landed on a German-occupied island in the Greek Aegean and walked to the Wehrmacht officers mess, opened the door and said to the astonished assembly, 'It would all be so much easier if you would just raise your hands.' Clark almost pulled the stunt off, but one quick-witted German grabbed a Luger pistol and started shooting. Luckily, Clark had brought his Glaswegian sergeant with him,' who promptly subdued the room with submachine-gun fire.

---

period in 1932 and the outbreak of war in 1939 were the toughest of his entire life.

But war was to change his life, as it changed the lives of everyone. Contemplating the mighty air force Hitler had assembled during the second half of the decade, Defence Staff found that their urgent need for pilots took priority over obscure gaps in King's Regulations, especially when the man in question had as much experience as Douglas Bader. They invited him back in, sent him on a refresher course, and on 27 November 1939 he found himself about to take off alone in an old Tutor biplane from the airfield at Upavon.

His friend and colleague Rupert Leigh remembered the occasion well. He was in his office when the telephone rang: it was the Chief Flying Instructor, Wing Commander Pringle.

Heroes

'Leigh! I have just passed a Tutor upside down in the circuit area at 600 feet. I know who it was. Be good enough to ask him not break all the flying regulations straight away.'

Bader was back.

His first station was Duxford, where he determined to behave himself and take his place as part of the team. The prevailing wisdom at the time was that fighter planes should attack in formation, so there was much emphasis on flying in tight patterns. Bader, determined that his positioning should be tighter and more accurate than anyone else's, was forced to crash land twice because he was so busy maintaining the precise 36-inch distance between his plane and his flight commander's that he failed to notice obstacles (a wooden hut and a tree) in his path. They were flying in Spitfires now, and avoidable accidents were frowned upon.

Nevertheless, he was soon appointed flight commander on 222 Squadron, where for the first time he had responsibility over other pilots in his flight. The promotion seemed to bring out the best in him. Enthusing his charges with his own passion for flying, he soon had them practising fighter attacks *his* way: in contrast with the stately processions (of sitting ducks, Bader thought) favoured by the Air Ministry, Bader had the Spitfires fight like guerrillas, waiting in ambush in the hidden places of the sky, then pouncing and engaging them in a furious dogfight in which surprise and the superior manoeuvrability of the Spitfire would be their trump cards. Under Bader's tutelage, his pilots became experts at aerobatics, hurling their aircraft around the skies and testing their capabilities to the limits – and sometimes beyond.

The war was frustratingly slow to come to the men of 222 Squadron. Day after day they trained, day after day they waited. Finally they were ordered to go and help provide cover for the evacuation at Dunkirk. On his first sorties, the enemy always seemed to be eluding him. Then at last they came across a flight of Messerschmitt 110s, heading menacingly for the long line of boats streaming back from Dunkirk. Bader threw open the throttle of his Spitfire and heard the howl of the Merlin engine as the aircraft surged in pursuit. Immediately, the 110s turned and headed back. A sixth sense made Bader look up, and there were four Messerschmitt 109s lurking in the shadows, preparing to dive. Then they fell on the line of Spitfires, angry bursts of red flashing from their machine-guns. Before they were past, Bader was wheeling after them. Although the 109 had greater straight-line speed, the British plane could turn on a sixpence, so that the 109s were at their most vulnerable when they closed for the kill. As he forced the stick over, a 109 appeared in his sights and he thumbed the firing button. The racket of the wing-mounted machine-guns filled his ears, then a puff of smoke from the German fighter. It staggered, there was a flash of orange from the cockpit, and the 109 lurched over, showing first the black cross on its side, then exposing its underbelly as it tumbled out of the sky.

Bader looked around, exultant, searching for another kill. But in that instant the skies had emptied, and there was nothing to do but turn for home. There, the news that two of his fellows had not made it home dampened his desire to relive the ecstasy of the kill.

There were more sorties over the Channel, but it was the other squadrons which always seemed to find the enemy. Once the evacuation was complete, they were back playing the waiting game. But Bader's leadership qualities and his nerve had not gone unnoticed. Despite overshooting the airfield during a night landing and pranging yet another Spitfire, Bader was made commander of 242 Squadron.

242 turned out to be a gang of unruly Canadians. They

had been heavily engaged in the rearguard over France as the Allied forces retreated north. During the chaos, they had become separated from each other, and had had to limp back home, dogfighting Luftwaffe planes by day, begging for fuel and a bed by night. Over a third had been killed, and more injured. They felt abandoned and demoralized, and disinclined to show any respect for a new British commander, let alone one with no legs.

Before addressing a word to any of them, Bader climbed unaided into the cockpit of a waiting Hurricane, took off, and for half an hour without respite he threw the aircraft around the sky in a breathtaking display of aerobatics, each routine merging flawlessly with the next. Showing off it may have been, but it was showing off with a purpose: none of his pilots ever doubted that Bader's disability was an irrelevance as far as flying was concerned.

Slowly, Bader won their confidence, using his charm and wit to draw them together again, make them feel pride in what they had done and eager for the fray. For hours on end he discussed tactics with them, preaching the virtues of the dogfight and listening to their experiences of combat: he was determined that they should fly formation as well as any, but equally insistent that when it came to the crunch, they should follow his less disciplined but more demanding approach. He fought tooth and nail for supplies, protected his men fiercely if they transgressed the official rules, and acted as focus and inspiration for the entire squadron.

The squadron was hardly operational before it was called south, to Duxford. The massed attacks of the Luftwaffe were about to begin.

'Two-four-two squadron scramble! Angels fifteen. North Weald.'

It didn't take long to find them, a formation of perhaps a hundred planes in all, Dornier bombers, Heinkels, 110s and 109s, blackening the skies as they thundered over Kent.

A Spitfire fighter plane used in the Battle of Britain

Heroes

Suddenly filled with savage fury at this invasion, Bader rolled his Hurricane and dived straight into the middle of a formation of Dorniers. The great bombers scattered as if pounded by a giant fist as Bader's Hurricane bellowed into their midst, guns spitting steel and flames. Once through, he was swinging up, seeking out the belly of a 110 and ripping it open with a long burst of fire. Up to his right, another 110 was swinging away in a slow turn and Bader was after it, the blood hot in his veins but mind and body taut with concentration as he poured every last ounce of skill and determination into making the kill. He was closing fast, oblivious to the seething skies around him, then jabbing the firing button, two quick bursts from behind. The Messerschmitt rocked from the impact, then a piece flew from its starboard wing and the stricken aircraft fell into a spin, flames spattering round its fuel tanks.

Bader searched the skies for another victim. But now a 110 had him in its sights, and tracer darted past his cockpit. Bader turned tight and fast until he had the 110 in his sights – but it was far below him now. He streaked in pursuit, but it was no good. The German plane was gone. The skies were deserted once more.

Back at base, 242 compared notes: twelve confirmed kills, several more damaged, and not so much as a bullet hole in any of the Hurricanes. Better still, not a single bomb had been dropped over Kent. Leigh-Mallory flew over to congratulate the squadron, and listened to Bader excitedly explaining how to break up a Luftwaffe bomber formation with just a handful of Hurricanes. In due course, Bader's tactic of simply diving into their midst became standard practice.

The calls to scramble soon started to come thick and fast as the Battle of Britain was closed in earnest. The Luftwaffe was under orders to pound Britain into submission in time for an autumn invasion, but the resistance was stout. Bader

Japanese 201st Air Group: Kamikaze!

On 25 October 1944 a Japanese Zero aircraft screamed out of the sky above Leyte Gulf, in the Philippines. Sailors in the American fleet below watched in paralysed horror as the Zero, guns blazing, dived straight at the carrier USS *Santee*, blowing an enormous hole in the flight deck. The Japanese suicide pilots had made their first attack. Dubbed 'Kamikaze', or Divine Wind in reference to the typhoon which saved Japan from invasion in the thirteenth century, the volunteer suicide pilots were a last desperate gamble to halt the US tide in the Pacific theatre. The pilots, who were treated as gods in Japan, drew for inspiration on the *Bushido* code of the old Samurai warrior class, especially its vaunting of the 'good death' in battle. Flying aircraft loaded with 550 lb bombs, the Kamikaze achieved spectacular successes, particularly after the introduction of the *kikusui* ('floating chrysan-themum'), which consisted of mass attacks by suicide bombers. During the battle of Okinawa, *kikusui* were responsible for the sinking of forty-four US vessels. Thereafter, to American relief, Japan simply ran out of aircraft to continue the Kamikaze attacks.

persuaded high command that it was pointless to keep squadrons in reserve: to face the huge formations of bombers and fighters, they needed to get amongst them with as many Hurricanes and Spitfires as possible, expose the clumsiness of the bombers and bring their own machine-guns to bear. Once, Bader was leading his squadron to intercept a bombing raid, but they came across the 'bandits' too early, before they had gained much height. Bader opened up the throttle and sent his powerful machine bellowing upwards; seeing the formation split-seconds later, not all of his pilots could keep up, and the squadrons behind were Spitfires, which climbed less strongly. Bader and two others broke into the Dorniers alone, firing at will but themselves under fire from innumerable tail gunners. Bader got another 110 in his sights and almost simultaneously caught sight of a 109 behind him. Delaying just long enough to get off a burst of machine-gun fire, he witnessed the puff of smoke from the German plane before breaking hard to the left. Then the Hurricane bucked and shuddered as tracer from the 109 smashed into it from behind. Fear clawed at Bader's heart, for the first time in his life. He was in a steep dive, cockpit full of smoke. *Bail out, for Christ's sake!* But as he got the cockpit hood open, the smoke cleared. It was only cordite from the machine-guns. Furious with himself for having been frightened, Bader roared in pursuit of another 110 and shot it down in flames. Then the sky was empty once again.

The squadron had taken heavy punishment that day – the other two had been so far behind they had virtually missed the fight, and 242 had taken them on alone. Several pilots were wounded and five Hurricanes had to be grounded. But between them they had eleven confirmed kills.

In between scrambles, Bader was pestering operations HQ to let him at the enemy sooner and more often and in greater numbers. Already at the head of three squadrons, now he was given five to lead into combat. In ordinary circumstances this would have been unthinkable, but the battle was a grim one, clearly a fight to the death, not only for the young pilots but perhaps for the nation as a whole.

If Hitler was able to invade, could the country withstand him? The young pilots of the RAF gave their lives daily to render the question irrelevant. It was death or glory . . . But death seemed always very close, and glory meant little when there was no time to bask in it. Tense and exhausted by the regular flirtation with death, elated and driven onwards by the sheer adrenalin-pumping thrill of the fight, living and dying on their nerves – it seemed impossible that the intense pitch of the fight could be maintained.

In such circumstances, a man like Bader was crucial to morale. His swashbuckling demeanour and absolutely unquenchable thirst for combat gave heart to those around him, particularly the younger pilots enduring a veritable baptism of fire. He was also developing an aura of invincibility in the air, and the pilots who flew with him felt that they shared in that aura and might be shielded from danger by his presence. Beyond his immediate colleagues, the fact that there was a man with no legs leading squadrons of Spitfires and Hurricanes against an enemy which outnumbered them by as much as ten to one was symbolic of the heroism being displayed by Fighter Command during those dangerous days. For fighter pilots throughout the RAF, here was a shining example of what could be achieved – even in the teeth of impossible odds – by dint of sheer determination, skill and courage. And for the townsfolk of the great cities of England, huddled at night under staircases or in cellars or under the kitchen table, the very existence of a hero like Douglas Bader was a source of inspiration, and people never tired of reading reports of his daring exploits in the pages of their newspapers.

Every time it engaged the enemy, 242 Squadron made around a dozen kills, and Bader was fifth in the RAF pecking order for number of confirmed kills. Unable to crack the extraordinary resistance of Fighter Command, Luftwaffe chief Goering began to vary his tactics, sending over decoys, trying to lure one of the groups of squadrons into the skies and away from the main thrust of the attack. The RAF adjusted accordingly, sometimes enjoying the rare delight of a dogfight in which they outnumbered the enemy, queuing up to shoot down the bombers and leaving the air full of German parachutes.

Leading the wing was the ideal place for Bader to be. Pipe clamped between his teeth, filling the radio waves with good-natured curses, he radiated the buccaneering spirit that made the RAF so formidable an opponent. His principal aim was always to scatter the bombers and down as many as possible, but he liked nothing better than to get in amongst the fighter screen of 109s, testing his flying skills and battle sense against the increasingly skilled German pilots, who had perfected their own tactic of diving in from on high, then screaming away from the battle before the Spitfires could engage them. The tactic, though eminently sensible, infuriated Bader, who claimed, to the delight of his fellow airmen, that the German pilots were scared of the RAF. And indeed, they had reason to be. The kill ratio remained hugely to their detriment, and there was something deeply unnerving about the way the Spitfires and Hurricanes hurled themselves against huge numbers of opponents, turning the might of the bombing formation into a hundred wild, nerve-jangling dogfights, spreading confusion and terror wherever they went.

There were many reasons why the Battle of Britain was won, but the *esprit de corps* of Fighter Command, its refusal to lie down and admit to defeat, and the aura of ferocity and invincibility it emanated – all these must have played a critical part. Morale is not easy to maintain when the rate of attrition is high and the war is not going the way you want it. That is when you need heroes most. Bader's career did not end with the Battle of Britain – he later went on numerous raids against German targets in France, was shot down and became a prisoner of war: in whatever PoW camp the Germans put him, he rapidly became a focal point for resistance or outright rebellion. It was in the man's nature to go on fighting no matter what the circumstances.

But his contribution to the Battle of Britain was his greatest achievement – and it was immense. The legend of the man who had no legs but went on hurling his Hurricane at the enemy until the enemy had had enough, who inspired a generation of young pilots to give their everything in a seemingly hopeless cause, who suffered cruelly but always came out fighting . . . This legend will always have a high place in the pantheon of heroic achievement.

El Alamein 1942

In North Africa, on 23–24 October 1942, General Montgomery's 8th Army of 200,000 men and 1,100 tanks, with commanding air support, attacked Field Marshal Rommel's Italians and Afrika Korps of 96,000 men and 500 tanks. Minefields and artillery held up the advance, and after five days the British had lost 10,000 men without achieving a breakthrough. Told to triumph, whatever the cost, Montgomery launched a further attack, which, assisted by RAF assaults, broke the enemy line and exposed their flanks. By 3 November Rommel was in retreat. The Axis forces were then pursued 1,500 miles by the British forces, who drove them from North Africa. Axis casualties were anything up to 10,000 men, with 30,000 taken prisoner. It was Britain's first land victory of the war, and raised shattered national morale.

Chapter Five

The Glorious Glosters & the Battle of the Imjin River

Any of you chaps happen to have a twist of tobacco to spare?
Lieutenant-Colonel James 'Fred' Carne

Sping arrives a little later in Korea than it does in England. But despite the unrisen sap the weather was mild as Padre S. J. Davies prepared his altar for Holy Communion in the ruin of a temple on a hill overlooking the Imjin River. It was Sunday, 22 April 1951, the day before St George's Day. Among the communicants was a young subaltern, Philip Curtis. Early the following morning he was killed charging a Chinese machine-gun nest.

Philip Curtis was a lieutenant of the Gloucestershire Regiment, one of the units Britain had contributed to the United Nations force assembled to repel communist North Korean forces from South Korea. The communists, urged on by the Soviet Union, had invaded in June 1950 and had been very close to success before the intervention of the United Nations (comprised in great majority of troops from the USA and under the command of the famous General MacArthur). The South Korean capital, Seoul, had been retaken in September, and by the end of October United Nations forces had occupied North Korea to within forty miles of the Chinese border.

The Chinese attacked, and in vast, irresistible numbers.

Heroes

Moreover, their military understanding of Korea's mountainous terrain was greater by far than the Americans', whose huge superiority in terms of armour and air power counted for little. They were caught in mountain passes by lightly armed but numerous Chinese forces using the methods of guerrilla warfare. The United Nations armies were pushed back relentlessly, evacuating Seoul in January 1951.

But the tide did turn, and the Allies reclaimed the South Korean capital in the middle of March. In early April United Nations troops dug in along the 'Kansas Line', more or less on the border of the two countries at the 38th Parallel (the line of latitude).

Some thirty miles north of Seoul, at the western end of the Kansas Line, 29 Brigade occupied an eight-mile front on the south bank of the Imjin River. To their west was a South Korean Division, to the east the Third Infantry Division of the American 1 Corps. 29 Brigade consisted of the Gloucestershire Regiment in the west, the Royal Northumberland Fusiliers in the centre and on the eastern flank a Belgian battalion. The Royal Ulster Rifles were in reserve. The 45th Field Regiment of the Royal Artillery provided artillery support.

United Nations forces had advanced cautiously to the Kansas Line, half expecting a Chinese counter-attack at any moment. However, on the morning of 22 April despite constant patrolling, there had been little evidence of enemy troops in numbers sufficient to suggest a major offensive. Seventy-two hours later the Gloucestershire Regiment had all but ceased to exist. Of the 741 men who had started the battle, 112 could be mustered immediately afterwards. Two Victoria Crosses were awarded, three DSOs and five Military Crosses. The Battle of the Imjin River became celebrated throughout the world.

The Glosters were made up of five companies. A

SAS Selection – What Makes a Hero?

Colloquially known as 'the Sickeners', the selection tests for the British Special Air Service (SAS) are amongst the toughest for any elite force. The Selection Training Course, based on one designed by Major John Woodhouse in 1950, runs for one with the emphasis on both physical and mental strength. Candidates begin with road runs and proceed to a number of rigorous cross-country marches carrying bergen rucksacks weighing up to twenty-five kilos. The culmination of the Selection Training Course is 'The Fan Dance', a sixty-kilometre land navigation over the Brecon Beacons in South Wales which has to be completed in twenty hours regardless of weather. By this stage a third of the candidates will have dropped out or been 'binned'. But this is not the end of the selection process – candidates still have to endure seven weeks of Continuation Training, which includes simulated interrogation by enemy intelligence forces, a five-day 'escape and evasion' test, where candidates have to live off the land equipped only with a knife and a box of matches, and parachute training. Successful candidates are then finally admitted to 'the Regiment'.

Company, commanded by Major Pat Angier, whose lieutenant was Philip Curtis, was in place on Castle Hill directly overlooking the Imjin. To their east, on a hill above the road that led south from the Imjin towards Seoul, was Captain Harvey's D Company. B (Major Harding) and C (Major Mitchell) Companies were on hill positions a mile south of the river, with the mountain of Kamak-San, some 2,000 feet high, to their rear. Support Company, under the command of Major 'Sam' Weller, provided mortars, heavy machine-guns and anti-tank services, and was deployed variously throughout the position. There was also a Pioneer Platoon, commanded by Captain 'Spike' Pike, an officer who had advanced through the ranks and was expecting orders to return to England at any time. Pike's men were comfortably dug in on Hill 235, at the rear of the battalion's position.

The Glosters occupied steep, rocky hills, but they were not precipitous, nor especially high. They were dry, covered in brushwood and odd outcrops of dwarf oak and sparse pine. The earth is reddish, but the landscape's only true colour was that of early-blooming azaleas, pink beneath the blue skies.

Some time after Padre Davies's service small groups of Chinese were spotted on the north bank of the river. The general feeling was that they were acting as a feint for a more substantial attack elsewhere along the line. But Lieutenant-Colonel James Power 'Fred' Carne, Commander of the Glosters, had a hunch that something grander was afoot. He felt that at the very least there would be a Chinese excursion across the river that night. He set an ambush at Gloster Crossing, the easy ford across which the Chinese could be expected to advance. Second-Lieutenant Guy Temple of C Company was given fifteen men, automatic weapons and plenty of ammunition. There was also a full moon.

As was his habit, Colonel Carne spent the evening hours of 22 April with those on watch in his command vehicle. At 10.20 he was informed that the Belgians, on the far right of the brigade's position and somewhat to the north, had come under attack. A few minutes later Temple rang in to say that a large number of Chinese was crossing the ford. The battle had begun.

Lieutenant-Colonel James Carne of the Gloucestershire Regiment

Heroes

Guy 'Guido' Temple was a shrewd choice. He was something of a rake, often hauled up for late returns from nightclubs back in England. He was also a decent draughtsman, whose drawings and paintings of the action accurately conveyed the chaos of battle. Now he was to prove himself 'a good man in a difficult time'.

Temple waited until the enemy were almost across the river before giving the order to fire. The Chinese went down in droves (the communist method of warfare being very much of the cannon-fodder school – almost a million Chinese troops were killed or wounded during the course of the Korean War). Temple reported breathlessly that 'At first it looked like ten or twenty coming across. We killed quite a few. Then I reckon hundreds of them were pouring across in the moonlight.' Temple's conduct both at Gloster Crossing and throughout the course of the battle were to earn him the Military Cross.

At brigade level the perception was that this attack and others like it along the brigade line were essentially probing efforts to gather information prior to a major offensive to come. What had not been realized was the ease with which the Chinese were crossing the Imjin at points other than fords or bridges. But as midnight passed the persistence of Chinese pressure all along the Allied line – 'like a swollen wave'* – indicated that their counter-offensive had begun in earnest.

On Castle Hill A Company was under fierce attack from both the north and, rather unexpectedly, from the west, the Chinese having crossed the river where there was supposed to be no crossing. Temple's men at the recognized ford, having repulsed four waves of Chinese, had to withdraw, having run out of ammunition. The Chinese poured through the breach and launched attacks on D Company. It

*Anthony Farrar-Hockley, *The British Part in the Korean War*, Vol. 2

was now that Colonel Fred Carne began to display the quietly heroic qualities that were to be so marked a feature of subsequent tales of the battle. Like an old-fashioned English policeman he was never seen to run. He never raised his voice, nor, most inspirationally, was his pipe ever seen to be removed from his mouth. Amidst the ferocious, almost suicidal onslaught of the Chinese, he seemed imperturbable, a kind of perfect English hero. To some, like Padre Davies, his nonchalance in the face of danger became 'almost irritating'.

By the morning of the 23rd hundreds of Chinese had been killed, but A Company had suffered very heavily. Over half the company had been killed or wounded, and the rest were exhausted, having fought continuously through the night. During the fighting the Chinese had taken the high ground on Castle Hill, and had placed a machine-gun nest on this point. A murderous spray issued from behind the mud walls of a former observation post. The gun had to be taken out.

Lieutenant Curtis's platoon was assigned the task. The difficulty lay in the terrain across which it would be necessary to advance. It was all open ground. Generous artillery support would have been nice but it was unavailable. All that was available was twenty tired, hungry men. The first attack was disastrous. Three men died in the first twenty yards, four more were wounded. Curtis decided that the only possibility of disabling the machine-gun post was for a single man to advance under covering fire from the others. He chose himself for the task. He made a little way before being severely wounded in the right arm and left side of his body. Some of his men, led by Corporal 'The Quack' Papworth (who received the Military Medal for his action in the battle) crawled out to bring him in, but before they could reach him he had resumed his charge. Bleeding profusely, carrying a revolver in one hand and a grenade in the other he managed to dodge the first deadly hail of fire from the machine-gun. When close enough he looped the grenade in a perfect lob towards the Chinese position. And as it looped Philip Curtis fell. One wonders whether he was aware of his success before he died.

Philip Curtis received a posthumous VC for his action. During the Second World War he had survived the blitz on Plymouth as a fourteen-year-old messenger for the ARP wardens; in 1943 he had tried to join the RAF but was told he was too young. He eventually served in the army for the final months of the war. He was twenty-five years old when he died. He left a motherless daughter to be brought up by her grandmother in Devonport.

Despite the heroism of Curtis and indeed all his comrades in A Company, their position could not be held. By now some thousand or so Chinese were attacking A and D companies. Even as Curtis charged the machine-gun Major Angier, Company Commander, was killed. In his last communication with Colonel Carne he had been told 'You will stay at all costs'. This was because withdrawal posed a grave threat to the western flank of the entire brigade position. Soon afterwards Carne was told that the threat had receded and that he could now withdraw his two beleaguered companies, and that a rifle company from the Royal Ulster Rifles was on its way to aid the operation.

However, Colonel Carne was aware that he could not afford to wait for the reinforcements to arrive (and in fact they never did). An artillery barrage was arranged, under cover of which A and D Companies began to withdraw southwards towards battalion HQ. It was ten o'clock in the morning. A couple of hours previously Carne had also redeployed B Company in order to maintain the integrity of his position, so outflanked were the Glosters in the east, so numerous were the Chinese in the valleys below. Carne was concerned that each company would be surrounded and destroyed one by one, and he wanted now to concentrate his forces in mutually supportive positions. It was 8.30 in the evening before the exhausted survivors of A and D had all staggered back through Battalion HQ. Major Angier's body had been brought back, his batman still inconsolable. The bodies of Lieutenants Curtis and Maycock had been irretrievable.

As evening approached on that 23 April, Padre Sam Davies stood in Battalion HQ, knowing that as soon as darkness fell the Chinese would attack again: 'the lonely battalion would be assaulted on all sides in the nightmarish moonlight. Gloucester was 11,000 miles away. I longed to be able to say "Stop" to the rushing minutes: to prolong this quiet, sunny afternoon indefinitely.'*

During the night of the 23rd/24th B Company was attacked seven times. By dawn ammunition was very low. When the grenades ran out the Chinese found themselves assailed by flying beer bottles. C Company too was under overwhelming pressure. Battalion HQ came under small-arms fire. It was time to move again. A and D Companies had already dug in on the highest ridge of Hill 235, and now it was imperative for the rest of the battalion to move in around them. From the old HQ position at the foot of the valley the hill was steep. Padre Davies abandoned his field Communion case. C Company too began to creep back towards positions within the new defensive perimeter which Carne had decided upon. The rest of the battalion watched from above as B Company, under constant fire, gingerly made its way back towards them. By the time the company reached its new positions it consisted of just seventeen men. The battalion itself had been reduced to some 300 fighting soldiers.

*S. J. Davies, *In Spite of Dungeons*

Heroes

Captain Anthony Farrar-Hockley, later to be Commander-in-Chief of Allied Forces in Northern Europe, was the Battalion Adjutant. As he stood next to his Commanding Officer, watching the arrival of B Company, Colonel Carne turned to him: 'It seems to me that you and I are going to find a job for ourselves as riflemen before very much longer.' Colonel Carne was true to his word. The following morning Farrar-Hockley was woken from a catnap by the sound of several grenade explosions. He investigated:

> Above me stood a group of machine-gunners and mortar-men; near by two signallers. They were all watching the Colonel. Armed with rifle and grenade he was completing the rout of a group of Chinese who had crept forward along the ridge – somehow unnoticed – in order to secure the knoll. Supporting him were two of the police and a driver.
>
> It was already over. Two Chinese soldiers lay dead about forty yards away and, a minute or so later, the Colonel was walking back, slinging the rifle over his shoulder as he came along towards me, filling his pipe.
>
> 'What was all that about, Sir?' I asked.
>
> He looked at me for a moment over the match that lit the pipe.
>
> 'Oh, just shooing away some Chinese,' he said.*

The Glosters' line had shrunk from five miles to 500 yards, concentrated on Hill 235, but it had not been pierced. Now Hill 235 was to become Gloster Hill, the site of the Battalion's last stand. Hearing Colonel Carne say as much a nearby mortar-man reassured him: 'We'll be all right sir – it'll be like the rock of Gibraltar up here.'

The Chinese tended to attack under cover of night, so there was time on the 24th, a 'fairly quiet day' according to

*Anthony Farrar-Hockley, *The Edge of the Sword*

Padre Davies, to attend to the wounded, bury the dead and prepare defences. The Chinese attacked sporadically, kept at bay by Lieutenant Cabral's snipers. At one point a fire started among the dry brushwood on the hillside. A detail had to be sent to beat it out.

On the 24th a determined attempt was made to relieve the beleaguered battalion by Centurion tanks of the 8th Hussars and elements of a Filipino infantry unit. The light tank that led the attempt was disabled, and the column ground to a halt. It was unlikely, however, that the heavier Centurions would have made much headway along the narrow road, and their shooting range would have been severely restricted. The column withdrew.

The plight of 29 Brigade as a whole was not properly recognized by the superior American commanders. This was due in no small part to the truth of Winston Churchill's maxim that the USA and the UK were two countries divided by a common language. When the American corps commander asked about the brigade's position he was informed by Brigadier Brodie that it was 'a bit sticky'. Any Briton would have recognized that this meant 'very bad'. The American took it at its literal meaning, 'mildly uncomfortable'. During the course of the battle Brigadier Brodie was twice told not to withdraw his brigade. At the same time he was denied sufficient air support and artillery to properly defend his positions.

To the east of the Glosters' position the Royal Northumberland Fusiliers and the Belgians had been similarly under attack by wave after wave of Chinese troops. The Belgians had been successfully withdrawn. During 24 April the Fusiliers too withdrew. For the Glosters any kind of formal withdrawal was looking increasingly impossible. They were surrounded. Nor had permission to make the attempt been granted. Brigadier Brodie, a veteran of the Second World War, was under no illusions as to the danger to his brigade. He had to fall back or risk being surrounded. In order to do so with some semblance of order it was necessary that the Glosters keep the Chinese occupied. Moreover he had been informed by his corps commander that an attempt to relieve the Glosters by units of the US Third Division had been cancelled. He called Carne during the afternoon. His message was 'Hold on where you are'. Carne and Brodie knew and liked one another, and Carne was calm as he made his reply to the Brigadier: 'I understand the position quite clearly. But I must make it clear to you that my command is no longer an effective fighting force. If it is required that we shall stay here, in spite of this, we shall continue to hold. But I wish to make known the nature of my position.' There was no more to say. The rest of 29 Brigade broke off from the enemy entirely and took up new defensive positions further south. Carne, having finished his conversation with Brodie, turned to his adjutant, Farrar-Hockley: 'You know that column that's coming from 3 Div to relieve us?'

'Yes, sir.'

'Well it isn't coming.'

'Right, sir.'

The Glosters were alone.

They must have looked a desperate band. They had had little sleep since the Sunday night. The last meal, consumed the previous evening, had consisted of a hard-boiled egg and a biscuit. Water was very low. The wireless batteries were running down. Helicopters tried to get through to pick up the wounded but could not penetrate the curtain of machine-gun fire that surrounded Gloster Hill. Supplies of ammunition and food dropped from aircraft fell out of reach. Artillery support, from the 45th Field Regiment, was dwindling as the gunners came under small-arms fire from the Chinese.

It is not necessary to be a student of strategy to grasp

the outline of the fighting that took place that night of the 24th. The Gloucestershire regiments were at the top of a hill, and the Chinese surrounded the bottom. The Chinese wanted to get to the top. From ten o'clock attacks were launched from three directions. These all failed. The Chinese attempted a series of permutations on these attacks. They too failed.

The strength of Chinese arms lay straightforwardly in their numbers, and an apparent willingness to throw life away with a minimum of concern. Despite massive casualties the onslaught increased rather than diminished. But human lives were all they had to hurl at their enemy. They had no air support, and little artillery. Nor did they have radios with which to communicate. Instead they used bugles. These bugles sounded continuously, and their weird eastern harmonics – 'slow and haunting in the sharp air' – must have been terribly grating on British ears. They certainly infuriated the Adjutant, Captain Farrar-Hockley. He yelled out of his shallow trench for Drum-Major Philip Buss to sound Reveille. Drum-Major Buss, a man with a huge moustache and the lungs to match, refused to sit in his trench to blow his horn, and so he stood, tall, lean, defiant. He played the long Reveille, the short Reveille, 'Cookhouse' (greeted with ironic cheers from hungry soldiers), 'Defaulters', 'Orderly NCO Calls', 'Officers Dress for Dinner', 'The Last Post', 'Lights Out', the American Reveille, and 'Taps'. Everything but 'Retreat'. And all the time the mortars fell, and machine-guns rattled, and rifle shots snapped back and forth.

In some places fighting was hand-to-hand. Mostly the Chinese were fought off from ten or twelve yards. Each bullet had to count. When it looked as though the Chinese were going to penetrate, covering fire was called for, at the risk of being shot by one's own side. The Glosters fought from thin trenches, and where the hard terrain made this

impossible they had built 'sangars' – little walls – out of
loose rock. The Chinese had no cover.

Battalion HQ all but ceased to exist on this last desperate
night of the battle. The Signals Officer, Captain Richard
Reeve-Tucker, was dead. The Assistant Adjutant,
Lieutenant Allman, though wounded, was commanding a
platoon. The Intelligence Officer, Lieutenant Cabral, was
leading another. The Adjutant himself, Anthony Farrar-
Hockley, with 'nothing to do' at HQ, led an attack by seventeen men of A Company on a little hill feature above their
positions: 'I look around the small body of men . . . I see that
it is a good lot of faces to be in a tight corner with.' They
took the feature. Later on, towards dawn, Colonel Carne
dropped in to Farrar-Hockley's trench. The Adjutant asked
the Colonel how things had been with him during the
night:

> He does not tell me that they have been under the most
> intense heavy machine-gun fire for the last fifty minutes; he
> does not admit to strolling about under fire along the whole
> front in order to visit and inspire companies; he does not say
> that he has made another sortie to repel a group of would-be
> infiltrators. He puffs at his pipe for a moment, regards the
> smoke drifting up into the air, and taps some ash back into
> the pipe bowl.
> 'Not bad really,' he says. 'Have you a match to spare?'*

Cometh the hour, cometh the man. Lieutenant-Colonel
Carne had previously given no special indication that
he was the stuff of which heroes are made. He was a
quiet, reserved man who had joined the Gloucestershire
Regiment in 1925. He had spent a large part of the Second
World War on the staff and in East Africa. Nor did he lose

*Anthony Farrar-Hockley, *The Edge of the Sword*

A few of the Gloucesteshire Regiment seen after fighting their way out of the Communist three-day encirclement

his taciturnity or his reserve as the napalm gushed around him at the Battle of the Imjin River. It became his strength. In all the published accounts of the battle his calm and his often unostentatious (often downright obvious) bravery are described as essential to the conduct of the battle. He had kept his men, throughout, from the horror of despair. He was awarded the VC in 1953 for 'powers of leadership which can seldom have been surpassed in the history of our Army'.

During the night of 24/25 April the Glosters gave not a foot of ground.

The fighting had been fierce and almost unrelenting but by morning, and in a brief lull, it was clear that the Glosters were no longer a military force. A Company had just three rounds left per man. At dawn Brigadier Brodie had called Carne and given him permission to break out. Colonel Carne called a final officers' conference. The battalion was to be informed that it should be ready to move at 10 a.m., and that 'every man is to make his own way back'.

There was not much choice as to what to do with the wounded. They would have to be left to the mercy of the Chinese. Captain Hickey, the regimental medical officer, who received the Military Cross for his bravery during the battle, did not need to be given any orders by his commanding officer. He said calmly that he 'quite understood the position'. Unhesitatingly, almost without thought, Padre Davies and Sergeant Brisland, the medical sergeant, volunteered to stay behind with him and his charges.

And so at 10 a.m. the Glosters broke into loose groups and began to look for ways through the ring of Chinese that surrounded them. Just before they left Fred Carne turned to Regimental Sergeant-Major Jack Hobbs, Corporal Strong and one or two others of his party: 'Any of you chaps happen to have a twist of tobacco to spare?'

As soon as the battalion had left Sergeant Brisland raised

the Red Cross flag and began to wave it vigorously. At that moment Drum-Major Buss, he of the moustache and the lungs, passed by. He stopped, horror-struck by what he regarded as a craven attempt to surrender a defensive position. He was swiftly informed by the Padre that the battalion had broken out and that he had better get a move on before he too was captured.

Almost all the surviving Glosters were captured. Only Captain Harvey and thirty-nine others, mostly members of D Company, made it back to United Nations lines, though not before having been fired at by American tank crews. The rest were all captured within twenty-four hours of the break-out. Naturally almost all had headed directly south towards the safety of the new United Nations line. But the degree to which the Glosters had been surrounded meant they would have had about as much chance of escaping had they gone north. The Glosters had been abandoned some sixteen miles behind enemy lines.

The stories of their captivity, and the heroism they displayed therein would fill a book. Second-Lieutenant Terry Waters of A Company received a posthumous George Cross, Padre Davies and Major 'Sam' Weller, Commander of the Support Company, both received the MBE, ten 'other ranks' the British Empire Medal.

A certain amount of controversy attaches to the battle of the Imjin River, and in particular to the Glosters' plight. While there is not much question that 29 Brigade as a whole had performed wonderfully, and essentially, to hold up the Chinese advance, it is questionable as to how necessary the Glosters' sacrifice was. It is said that they could have been withdrawn earlier or relieved effectively. Blame seems to have been distributed throughout the higher commanders in Korea, from brigade to corps to army. Insofar as the war was concerned, the Battle of the Imjin River was a victory, but what happened to the Glosters an unnecessary tragedy.

Heroes

There is not room for mention of the parts played by all the heroes of this action, of Major Harding (who received the DSO), of Major Grist (OBE), of Warrant-Officer Hobbs (MBE), of Captains Mardell and Harvey and Martin and Lieutenant Costello (all MCs), of the ten sergeants and corporals and privates who received the Military Medal, of the dozens who were mentioned in despatches. Nor should the presence of C Troop of the 170th Independent Mortar Battery be forgotten.

The heroism of the Glorious Glosters was recognized at once, not least in the United States. The *New Yorker* published a long and gripping despatch. The *Boston Globe* gave over an entire front page to the battalion. A Presidential Citation was conferred, which concluded with these words: 'Their sustained brilliance in battle, their resoluteness and extraordinary heroism are in keeping with the finest traditions of the renowned military forces of the British Commonwealth and reflect unsurpassed credit on these courageous soldiers and their homeland.'

But perhaps the last words should go to Anthony Farrar-Hockley, who received the DSO (to add to an MC won in Italy) for his own part in the action:

> *After his orders to the battalion to break out, Brigadier Brodie entered in the brigade operations log in a moment of high emotion, 'No one but the Glosters could have done it.' This was flattering but not true. The other members of the brigade fought no less well. Neither they nor the Glosters sought to be heroes; only to acquit themselves honourably and competently, one among the other.*
>
> *That is the best of the soldier's calling.**

---

*Anthony Farrar-Hockley, *The British Part in the Korean War*, Vol. 2

Chapter Six

Colonel 'H' Jones

The Falklands War, conducted so far away from the British Isles, was always going to be an extremely high-risk campaign, where resources and endurance would be stretched to the extreme, and the margin between success and defeat never anything but precariously small. Every advantage, however slight, had to be seized upon. Every facet of the British forces had to contribute their utmost and the number of medals awarded to servicemen of all ranks is a clear indication of how courageously the challenge was met. But the greatest renown has been granted to one particular medal – the Victoria Cross – and the specific acts of heroism and self-sacrifice performed by one forty-two-year-old man – Lieutenant-Colonel 'H' Jones, the Commanding Officer of the 2nd Battalion of the Parachute Regiment. The role 'H' Jones played in the war was brief, in terms of time, and its denouement came a week after landing. But, apart from influencing the outcome of the first vital infantry engagement, his fearless determination and will to win made an indelible impression on the whole war. His leadership, his gallantry and his extreme bravery both inspired and became a symbol of the superiority that propelled the British to victory. Once that sense of superiority was secure in British minds and hearts, they were formidable opponents, no matter how far from home they found themselves and ensuring this was perhaps 'H' Jones's greatest achievement.

The decoying tactics the British used to suggest that they were going to make a landing at Port Stanley were completely successful and there was no reception committee when, on the night of 21 May 1982, the troops of 3 Commando Brigade piled off their troopships and into the landing craft in San Carlos Water. The 2nd Battalion of the Parachute Regiment – better known as 2 Para – led the way, plunging, heavily loaded with equipment, into the freezing water and then setting off up Sussex Mountain, the steep hill that dominated the landscape around San Carlos. Respite, however, was short-lived, because on 22 May the Argentinian Air Force discovered the landing and began a harrowing five days of bombing raids on the British fleet. On 22 May HMS *Antrim* and HMS *Ardent* were hit and the latter was sunk. On 23 May, a Sunday, HMS *Antelope* was hit, exploding late that day and sinking on the next. On 24 May, which came to be known as 'Bomb Alley Day', the Commando Brigade Headquarters, HMS *Fearless*, was hit by a rocket, two bombs ploughed into *Sir Launcelot* without exploding and the logistics ship, *Sir Galahad*, was hit and abandoned.

Considering that they were without air cover and hadn't had time to set up mines or wires, it was extremely lucky that the British infantry did not come under air or land attack during this period. But it was still a frustrating and disturbing time, forced to witness the relentless bombardment of the navy, without knowledge of the number of Argentinian planes shot down by the British and without any clear plan of when or how they were going to break out of the beachhead. With typical black humour, comparisons were made with Gallipoli and the Crimea, but there was a mounting seriousness behind their jokes. Their frustration was mirrored by growing political pressure in Britain for something to happen on land, and on 24 May it was decided that troops would be helicoptered forward to the hills surrounding Port Stanley, so that they could get on with taking the town and fulfilling the war's main objective.

A subordinate plan, to take the Argentinian garrison at Goose Green, which had been proposed and backed up by a preliminary SAS raid, was dropped. Everything, however, had to be changed when 25 May turned out to be the worst day of bombing yet, claiming almost the entire complement of helicopters taken to the Falklands. HMS *Coventry* was hit and sunk, HMS *Broadsword* was hit and, most disastrously of all, the supply ship *Atlantic Conveyor* was hit by an Exocet missile. Enough tentage and living equipment for 10,000 troops, a mile of portable steel runway and nine helicopters, including three of the massive Chinook helicopters, went down with it, and from then on the infantry had to get round the Falklands on foot. 'Yomping' was set to enter the English vocabulary.

To their considerable dismay, therefore, Brigade Head-quarters was forced to resurrect the Goose Green plan. 2 Para were entrusted with the job of capturing the Argentinian garrison and airbase, and liberating the Falklanders held there and in the settlement at Darwin. Two other infantry units – 45 Commando and 3 Para – were to set off for Port Stanley on foot, 42 Commando were to follow later and 40 Commando were entrusted with the defence of San Carlos. Strategically, it was not an ideal step to have to take. To have to commit one of only five infantry units in an engagement on the flank and so early in the campaign. To send them heavily laden on a long approach march across difficult country, without vehicles, with only limited helicopter lift and with no guarantee of avoiding air or land attack. Above all, to entrust them with an objective, where they had civilians' safety to think of, where the ground was open and afforded them no cover, and where they had no clear idea of the Argentinians' strength, apart from the knowledge that they had had plenty of time to lay minefields and dig themselves in in prepared positions. None of these were decisions that any officer would have taken with any enthusiasm. There were few arguments conclusively in favour of the battle for Goose Green. The Argentinian garrison there might pose a threat to San Carlos. It could be beneficial to hit the Argentinians hard and quickly. Most persuasively of all 2 Para were only too eager and none more so than their Commanding Officer 'H' Jones.

'H' Jones was on a family skiing holiday when the Argentinians invaded the Falklands and he immediately drove back to England to argue for 2 Para's inclusion in the Task Force. Throughout his eminent military career, the opportunity to lead his battalion in war was what he had always been waiting for. Educated at Eton and Sandhurst, and commissioned into the Devon and Dorset Regiment, he was awarded an MBE in 1971 for his service as Brigade Major of the Third Infantry Brigade in Northern Ireland. This was followed by an OBE for his role in planning the peace-keeping force in Zimbabwe and in April 1981 he took command of 2 Para, a battalion that sought in every way to uphold the traditions of the Parachute Regiment and the legacy of Arnhem. 'H', as he was known by everybody – he disliked his Christian name Herbert and insisted on the abbreviation – not only fitted in immediately, but set a new example and new standards. An enthusiast and keen sportsman, supremely fit and an excellent shot, 'H' was the model of a leader who leads from the front. Charming and good-looking, his sole concern, however, was the good of his battalion. He could be hard on those who fell short of his demands, compromise was not a part of his nature and his first instinct was always to get involved, to observe and get things done himself. In the first days after landing, for instance, there was every chance that he would be in the forward observation posts rather than where most people expected to find him, in his headquarters. But these were the qualities that had deeply impressed 2 Para and incurred their lasting respect and trust. Here was a leader who could be relied upon, whatever the danger and risk to his personal safety, to do his duty and uphold the battalion's honour to the utmost.

In 'H's opinion, the operation had only a 75 per cent chance of success. An amphibious approach to the south of Goose Green, with the dangers of submerged rocks and mines, was consequently ruled out and on 26 May, 2 Para set out, marching fast towards Camilla Creek House, a farmhouse eight miles away that had been used as an enemy observation post. Shelling started up after they got under way, suggesting that perhaps they had been spotted, but the shells fell far to the left and they reached the farmhouse and spent the night there safely. To everyone's incredulity, the BBC World Service then broadcast that a parachute battalion was poised and ready to assault Darwin and Goose Green, but that too seems not to have endangered their position and the great part of 27 May was spent laid up at the farmhouse while reconnaissance patrols observed the Argentinians. These retreated when they came under Argentinian fire and, as evening fell, 'H' convened the Orders group, or 'O' group, where he outlined his strategy for the forthcoming battle.

By any standards, it was a formidable task. Darwin and Goose Green lie on the south side of an isthmus that is five miles long and no more than about a mile wide. Halfway down the isthmus is a spine, a thick gorse line that runs from the ruined Boca House in the east to the hilltop overlooking Darwin in the west. The ground is extremely irregular, with small rises and gullies, and utterly bare and windswept, dotted only with small hummocks of gorse. The chances of outflanking the Argentinians, therefore, were extremely small and the element of surprise had been lost when the reconnaissance patrols were spotted. 2 Para had little artillery support. Three 105 mm light guns of 8

Heroes

Commando Battery, which were airlifted just to the north of Camilla Creek House, 81 mm mortars and HMS *Arrow*'s one 4.5 inch gun, along with air cover that would commence at first light. The rest of the artillery was needed to defend the other infantry units heading towards Port Stanley and it was decided that tanks wouldn't be used because of the lack of firm tracks. The final drawback was the lack of exact knowledge of the Argentinians' positions and strength. A rough picture had been put together from the reconnaissance missions, but it was not known that the Argentinians had the equivalent of a reinforced battalion, including the high-quality troops of C Company of the 12th Regiment of the Argentinian Army. 2 Para went into battle outnumbered three to one.

Given all these constraints, 'H' decided that the operation would be split into six individual phases and, overall, into two sections. The first and most important would be a night attack, a sustained sweeping movement from the north where 2 Para's four companies would drive down the isthmus, rolling over the Argentinian positions and clearing their troops out of Darwin and Goose Green by daylight. A Company would head down the east coast to Darwin and B Company down the west to Boca House, only one company would be engaged at any one time and the others would be held in reserve, ready to work their way round the edge if the leading company got held up. If all went to plan, the second section of the battle would be the protection of the civilians in Goose Green during the morning of 28 May. Speed and momentum, therefore, were of the utmost importance. At no stage could the attack be allowed to get bogged down or the initiative lost.

The 'O' group, therefore, had to be kept as short as possible. A Royal Marine officer, Lieutenant John Thurman, who had served in the Falklands before, gave details of the terrain and Captain Allen Coulson, the Intelligence Officer, briefed 2 Para's officers on the Argentinian positions. But both their descriptions had to be curtailed, there was a shortage of maps and most critically, the group of trenches spotted by one of the reconnaissance patrols on a small rise that came to be known as Darwin Hill were not included in the officers' information. There was no time to delay, since there was still a four-and-a-half-mile march to the Start Line. This was covered at top speed and, on the morning of 28 May, A Company crossed the Start Line at Zero Hour – 3.30 a.m. local time. B and D Companies followed them half an hour later. The battle for Goose Green had begun.

Night attacks had long been a staple of NATO exercises because of the strength of the Russian Air Force but practice alone does not diminish their essential difficulty as manoeuvres. Apart from being freezing cold, it was a very dark night and it soon began to rain. The first objective, the Argentinian positions presumed to be based at Burntside House in the north-east of the isthmus, were unproblematic. 2 Para raked the building with bullets until shouting from inside revealed that the Argentinian platoon had fled and left behind the house's owner, a shepherd, his wife, his mother and a friend. Better news came when there turned out to be no trees planted across the narrow neck of the isthmus, which would have been an ideal defensive tactic if the Argentinians had not been planning for a seaborne attack. But visibility was so poor and the need to keep up a fast pace was so imperative that things soon became very confusing. Companies bypassed machine-gun positions without realizing it and then, just as suddenly, came across others. Platoons got split up and lost contact with each other. Only the great courage and initiative of individual platoon commanders, the comparatively low quality of Argentinian troops at this stage of the battle and the overall level of aggression kept the British momentum going. The first Argentinian prisoners taken were mainly rear-echelon troops, such as cooks, and many of their soldiers went into traumatic shock, hiding at the bottom of their trenches in foetal positions. Meanwhile, all the British ranks fought bravely, as can be seen from the Military Medals awarded to Lance-Corporal Gary Bingley and Private Barry Grayling for their attack on a four-man Argentinian machine-gun post.

While B Company moved down the right flank, A Company were making good headway down the left, and their Commander, Major Dair Farrar-Hockley, left one platoon on Coronation Hill before setting off to encircle the tiny settlement of Darwin, which was now less than a mile away. He had time to consult with 'H', who urged him to keep pushing on in the belief that the main Argentinian positions had now been breached. The situation, at this stage, was looking very good and the attack seemed to be on, if not ahead of, schedule.

As A Company moved forward, they saw a small rise ahead of them and on it, three unarmed men who were waving at them. For one surreal moment of misunderstanding, the two groups faced each other. The British thought that perhaps they were civilians out walking their dogs. The Argentinians thought that the British were retreating Argentinians. Suddenly both sides realized their mistake and the British came under heavy fire, instinctively running for cover either at the dead ground right at the foot of the hill or in the gorse gulley to its left. It was 6.45 a.m. local time, and the only day-long battle of the war had started.

Far from having driven through the Argentinians' defences, the British had only now reached their main defence position, a line of twenty-three trenches across the rise soon to be known as Darwin Hill and a small rise to the west. The trenches further forward had only ever been intended as buffers, with inferior troops who were ready to retreat to the gorse line and join the company already

Colonel 'H' Jones, hero of the Falklands War

occupying it. Ninety-two men, in all, were dug in and the British were in a very difficult position, pinned down on very bare ground right under the Argentinians' noses just as it was starting to get light. Artillery fire would have helped, but at first they seemed too close to the Argentinians to risk it and anyway, the guns were needed by B Company, which, by now, was pinned down by a machine-gun post at Boca House. When Farrar-Hockley eventually did call up artillery fire, the firing was too inaccurate and he had to call it off. The Harriers couldn't provide an air strike because fog at sea was preventing them taking off and, as has been pointed out before, there were no tanks on hand. The only option, therefore, seemed to be to wear the Argentinians down slowly by individual skirmishing actions.

'H' and his Battalion Headquarters had been following behind A Company and they had taken cover when the firing broke out from Darwin Hill. For him personally and for his battalion plan, this hold-up was absolute anathema. He wanted it solved quickly and, to do so, he wanted to find out exactly what was going on. First-hand experience was his life blood. He always wanted to be well forward and, if there was a major threat to the progress of the whole battalion, he wanted to dispel it by personal intervention and example. Other options did present themselves. Major Philip Neame suggested that he had found a way for D Company to outflank Boca House to the west, for example. But that sort of solution, so far from where 'H' found himself in the battle, held little appeal and he firmly told D Company to stay where it was. Instead he decided to join A Company and, typically, having made the decision, he immediately set off at a furious pace, hurling smoke grenades to distract Argentinian fire and sprinting across the dangerously exposed ground. He reached Farrar-Hockley at 8.30 a.m.

It is hard to imagine what it must have been like at the foot of Darwin Hill where A Company had now been pinned

SAS: The Hardest Day

In July 1972 nine men of the British SAS were attacked by 250 communist guerrillas at Mirbat, in the Sultanate of Oman. Completely surrounded, the fortified base (the 'Batthouse') of the SAS was subjected to withering fire by 75 mm recoilless rifles, mortars, heavy machine-guns and even a Carl Gustav 84 mm rocket launcher. Though the SAS Commanding Officer, Mike Kealy, had never been in action before, he, along with Corporal Bradshaw, organized a devastating pattern and rate of return fire which chopped away at the advance of the guerrillas. At one stage, though, the guerrillas were so close that the SAS mortar-man had to support the mortar barrel with his legs in a near-upright position. Several SAS men, including Kealy, made dashes amid the bullets to a nearby gunpit, to operate a 25 pounder belonging to the Sultan's gendarmerie. While Kealy was in the gunpit a grenade rolled in – but failed to explode. Minutes later Strikemaster jets of the Sultan's Air Force screamed in at low level, cannons firing, and the guerrillas began to withdraw. The siege was over. For the loss of two men, the SAS had survived its hardest test.

down for nearly two hours. Perhaps 'H' felt the whole battle was in jeopardy. More likely, he thought that the Argentinian trenches were an obstacle that must not be allowed to dominate the British. Nothing was going to stand in their way. He would not permit it. Taking his time to acclimatize, therefore, he thought through the various possibilities. He suggested several manoeuvres, all of which were immediately ruled out. He then ordered a charge up the hill to set up a fire team. The men set off, but Captain David Wood, the Battalion Adjutant, Captain Chris Dent, A Company's Second in Command and Corporal David Hardmann were killed immediately and the rest fell back. An hour after reaching A Company, 'H's leadership seemed to be facing its critical test. The death of three of his officers must have been a very hard blow. The frustration at the lack of progress, despite all his efforts, must have been intolerable. Perhaps he felt that one last assault would be enough, after he had brought his men this far, after he had yearned for so long to lead them to glory in battle. Perhaps all his deepest instincts, his profound fearlessness, pride and sense of overall reponsibility coalesced in an instant of extreme clarity. No one can presume to know what exactly goes through a soldier's mind at the height of battle. What is incontrovertible is the course of action 'H' then took.

Deciding personally to lead a flanking movement round the right-hand side of Darwin Hill, 'H' shouted out instructions – which ones is not exactly clear, but they were along the lines of 'Follow me!' – and then sprinted off up the re-entrant towards the nearest line of trenches. Seeing him set off, his bodyguard, Sergeant Barry Norman, grabbed his gun and ran after him. As he rounded the hill 'H' was already firing at the trenches with his Sterling submachine-gun. Finishing one magazine, 'H' crouched down to reload a fresh one and then launched a second attack. What he hadn't seen was the trench thirty yards behind him that was the first in the next line of Argentinian trenches running inland. 'H' was caught between the two sets of trenches, his solitary figure exposed against the bare ground, he could not have presented an easier target. When the firing started, he was hit immediately in the back. Sergeant Norman was too far behind to cover him, but he reached him soon after he fell and dragged him into cover. At 9.30 a.m, 'H's radio operator broadcast the message, 'Sunray is down.' At 10 a.m. on 28 May 1982, Lieutenant-Colonel 'H' Jones OBE died without regaining consciousness. Within fifteen minutes, the seventy-four surviving Argentinian soldiers left their trenches waving white cloths.

Major Chris Keeble, 2 Para's Second in Command, was by no means in an easy position when 'H's death forced him to take over command – seemingly stymied on both flanks, in full daylight and only halfway towards achieving the battalion's objective. He gave the go-ahead to D Company to start outflanking Boca House and, in conjunction with B Company's Milan anti-tank launchers, they started to lay down an invincible field of fire. But, although 'H's solo charge had been undertaken without fully informing his officers what he was doing, his heroism prompted a definitive response. While 2 Platoon fought round the left and distracted the Argentinians' attention, two NCOs of 3 Platoon worked themselves into a position to aim a 66 mm anti-tank rocket launcher at the trench from which 'H' had been hit. Sergeant Terry Barret fired first and missed. Corporal David Abols then fired and scored a direct hit. After this decisive strike, they worked their way through the trenches, which could not cover each other because they were not staggered. In no time the Argentinians surrendered and Sergeant Barry was awarded a Military Medal, while Corporal Abols was awarded a Distinguished Conduct Medal.

With the surrender of the machine-gun post at Boca House, the initiative was now firmly back on the British side and it was not lost for the rest of the battle. Darwin was encircled, heavy fighting broke out round the schoolhouse and other buildings on the outskirts of Goose Green and, as evening fell, three GR3 Harriers delivered a devastating cluster bomb attack on the Argentinian artillery positions. This may have been the final blow that broke Argentinian resistance.

Under cover of darkness both sides reinforced themselves. The Argentinians were still the superior force in terms of numbers and ammunition, but their every attempt to hold up the British advance had failed and now they had even less room to manoeuvre. Negotiations lasted throughout the night, but on the morning of 29 May they surrendered and, after fifteen hours of continuous fighting, the battle for Goose Green was over.

The first conflict on land, the only engagement in the whole campaign to take place in daylight and the only one to involve civilians, none of whom were harmed, the battle for Goose Green was obviously of immense significance. The British victory had a resounding influence, not only for its comprehensiveness, but, supremely, for the way in which it was won. 2 Para – numbering 500 – had defeated 1,500 Argentinian soldiers. According to official British figures, forty-seven Argentinians and seventeen British soldiers had died, of which four were officers, seven were junior NCOs and one was the Commanding Officer.

Perhaps there is no better way to characterize the achievement of 2 Para, in general, and of 'H' in particular, than to quote from his Victoria Cross citation: 'They [2 Para] achieved such a moral superiority over the enemy in this first battle that, despite the advantage of numbers and selection of battle-ground, they never thereafter doubted either the superior fighting qualities of the British troops, or their own inevitable defeat. This was an action of the utmost gallantry by a commanding officer whose dashing leadership and courage throughout the battle were an inspiration to all about him.' 'H' is buried in the Falklands, his grave, like his life, a tribute to the unquenchable fire of heroism that, even in modern warfare, still burns bright.

Chapter Seven

James Wolfe & the Battle for Quebec

He looked upon danger as the favourable moment that would call forth all his talents.

Horace Walpole on James Wolfe, 1757

It is quite possible that at 2 a.m. on the morning of 13 September 1759, floating down the St Lawrence River in a flat-bottomed boat, General James Wolfe recited Thomas Gray's great poem 'Elegy written in a Country Churchyard' to the officers around him. Having finished he is reported to have said: 'I can only say, gentlemen, that, if the choice were mine, I would rather be the author of these verses than win the battle which we are to fight tomorrow morning.' It is generally thought that the verse that prompted the General was:

> *The boast of heraldry, the pomp of power,*
> *And all that beauty, all that wealth e'er gave*
> *Awaits alike th'inevitable hour.*
> *The paths of glory lead but to the grave.*

But it may have been another famous verse which ends with the line: 'They kept the noiseless tenor of their ways'. Wolfe had given orders for silence as the huge flotilla carrying his army made its way downriver towards the Anse de Foulon at the foot of the Heights of Abraham. At the top lay Quebec, devastated but unconquered and quite unprepared for an attack from this quarter. The Heights of Abraham rise almost sheer for 250 feet. A desultory French picket of about one hundred men guarded the steep path that zigzagged up from the Anse.

British troops started filing up the narrow track at around 4 a.m. By 10.30 the French had been defeated, Quebec and Canada lay at the mercy of the British and James Wolfe was dead. He had indeed met his 'inevitable hour'. He was thirty-two years old.

James Wolfe was born in 1727, at Westerham in Kent. He was the son and grandson of army officers. There was never any question as to what occupation he would pursue. He saw his first action at the age of fourteen, and had a horse shot from under him at the battle of Dettingen in 1743, during the War of Austrian Succession. In 1745 he was sent to Scotland and took part at the battles of Falkirk and Culloden.

During the course of the next ten years Wolfe won a reputation as a first-rate officer. He was a zealous improver both of self and of those he commanded. He realized that soldiers, in order to be effective to the highest degree, needed to be highly disciplined. But he also realized that good discipline rested not on fear but on content. In other words he made sure that his soldiers were healthy, well-fed, comfortable in their uniforms, and equipped with the best armaments.

But in an age when promotion in the British Army depended on birth, favour, corruption or a combination of all three, Wolfe had no powerful influences to ease his rise. While the idleness and ignorance of the officer class made Wolfe's proficiency and zeal all the more marked, they were also qualities that made him unpopular among his colleagues.

In the event merit was to be given its due by the accession

William Pitt

to power in 1757 of political genius in the form of William Pitt.

The Seven Years War broke out in 1756. It arose from the attempt by Austria to win back land lost to the Prussians in the War of Austrian Succession. The Austrians formed a powerful coalition involving France, Russia and Sweden. British involvement centred, at least to begin with, on a desire to protect Hanover, but Pitt saw an opportunity to take on the French in further flung corners of the world, specifically North America and India.

Pitt recognized that Great Britain was essentially a mercantile and maritime power, and that her weapons were her fleet and her wealth. So far as Europe was concerned the strategic imperatives were to keep open the Channel and the Mediterranean, and to provide Frederick the Great of Prussia with any necessary funding. A small Anglo-Hanoverian Army under Cumberland was maintained on the Continent. At the same time Pitt realized that the French could be kept busy on two fronts by harassing actions on her Atlantic coast. One of these actions was directed against Rochefort at the mouth of the Charente, and it was here that Wolfe earned himself the praise which led eventually to his unlikely command (given his age and lack of influence) of the expedition to Quebec two years later.

Rochefort was a failure. Horace Walpole described the man chosen to lead it, a General Mordaunt, as 'broken in spirit and constitution', and that was before the fleet sailed. Wolfe, who was appointed Quartermaster General, had his own misgivings: 'the chiefs, the engineers & our own wretched discipline are the great and insurmountable obstructions,' he wrote. These comments find their complement in Walpole's opinion of Wolfe himself: 'a young officer who had contracted a reputation from his intelligence of discipline, and from the perfection to which he had brought his regiment'.

Wolfe was furious at the failure in France. But on the strength of his part he was at last promoted to colonel. In the following year he was appointed one of three brigadiers to serve under Major-General Amherst for an attack on Louisbourg, the French fortification at the north of Nova Scotia which allowed control of shipping in and out of the Gulf of St Lawrence.

New France had grown steadily in the first half of the century, to such an extent indeed that British trade around the Hudson Bay was being damaged. The French also made inroads into Ohio, which more or less confined British traders to the eastern seaboard. In 1753 a certain George Washington led an army to reclaim British land in Ohio. He was defeated. As a consequence British regular troops were sent to America in substantial numbers, though by 1756 they had made little headway.

Now, with Pitt at the helm, the British prepared to force the issue once more. Pitt bad a three-point strategy for the conquest of New France. Fort Duquesne in the south and Louisbourg on the coast were to be the first two targets. From thence the two British armies would move on Montreal and Quebec.

General Amherst was appointed to command the expedition, and he was in personal charge at Louisbourg. A proficient administrator but an indifferent soldier, he took far too long about his task, and although Fort Duquesne was taken by General Forbes (renamed Pittsburgh) the opportunity to attack Montreal and Quebec had passed.

Louisbourg made Wolfe a star, 'The Lion of Louisbourg'. His own part had been played in an exemplary fashion. Indeed it was generally perceived that his qualities as a leader had more or less saved the expedition from disaster.

By December 1758 Pitt had hatched a new plan for an attack on Montreal and Quebec. Wolfe, back in Britain, was invited to an interview with Lord Ligonier, Commander-in-Chief of the Army in Great Britain. Wolfe reported afterwards: 'We had some discourse concerning the navigation of the River St Lawrence, and upon the project of besieging Quebec, and I found it was a settled plan to carry on two separate attacks, one on the side of Lake St George, and one up the river.' Wolfe was given the 'one up the river', Amherst the other. As naval commander Pitt appointed Charles Saunders, a man described by Horace Walpole as 'a pattern of the most sturdy bravery'. Wolfe was delighted.

Wolfe was given the rank of major-general. There was considerable objection from the more established elements in the army. George II was informed that Wolfe was 'mad'. 'Mad is he?' puffed the old warrior King, 'then I hope he will bite some of my other Generals.'

Under him Wolfe had three brigadiers, two of whom he chose himself.

His second in command was the Honorouble Robert Monckton, a son of Lord Galway, who had served for six years in North America and was an experienced and competent soldier.

The second brigadier was the Honourable George Townshend. Townshend was a man of some influence. Walpole discribed him as 'proud, sullen and contemptuous'. But he was also a man of intelligence and talent. During the battle of Dettingen, where Townshend, like Wolfe, was still in his teens, a drummer boy standing nearby him had had his head smashed to pulp by a cannon ball. A veteran soldier sought to reassure the young man. 'Oh, I'm not afraid,' Townshend had responded, 'I'm only astonished that a fellow with such a quantity of brains should be here.' His watercolour portrait of Wolfe at Quebec is generally considered the best likeness available to us. He was also a cartoonist, with the cartoonist's cruel eye, and several caricatures of his Commanding Officer did the rounds while the British Army laid siege to Quebec. Townshend was not one of Wolfe's own choices.

Fourth in command was James Murray. A subordinate officer described him as 'the very Bellows of sedition; envious, ambitious, the very mention of another's merit canker'd him'. But Wolfe had a high estimate of Murray's 'spirit', which was, to Wolfe, the highest quality a soldier could have.

Wolfe's army was supposed to be 12,000 strong but in the event it numbered some 8,500. They were, however, good soldiers. At his disposal Wolfe had ten British line battalions, a battalion of Louisbourg Grenadiers, three companies of Royal Artillery and six companies of American rangers. Admiral Saunders's fleet consisted of eleven sail-of-the-line and some 120 transports, ordnance vessels and victualling ships. All in all it was a powerful force.

On 17 February Saunders sailed from Spithead in the *Neptune*. Wolfe's intention was to muster all his forces at Louisbourg on 20 April, but storms and ice held the fleet up, and the assembly did not come about until the middle of May.

In the meantime a French fleet had got to Quebec carrying supplies, ammunition and a few reinforcements. It also brought back a young officer named Bougainville, who was later to circumnavigate the globe, serve under Napoleon, and introduce the bougainvillea into Europe. By the time of Quebec he had already been elected a Fellow of the Royal Society in London for his work on calculus. For good measure he had a degree in Law. He had gone to Paris to plead the colonists' cause, but was told that 'when the house is on fire [in other words, France], one doesn't bother about the stables'. He famously replied: 'At least no one will say you talk like a horse.' To Montcalm, commanding the French forces, it is likely that Bougainville alone was more important than the meagre reinforcements he had returned with.

Montcalm himself was a man of good birth and high reputation as a professional soldier. He was fifteen years older than Wolfe, and a deal less intense. His manner of command was sardonic, cheerfully pessimistic, but never less than soldierly. He disliked being abroad and yearned for his family and his home. In his last letter to his wife he wrote: 'I think I would give up all my honours to be back with you, but the King must be obeyed. The moment I see you again will be the best of my life.' That moment never came.

Nor did his relationship with the Governor of New France, the Marquis de Vaudreuil, help matters. Vaudreuil fancied himself possessed of a sharp military mind and disliked any suggestion that he might be in the wrong. Bougainville had brought back a letter from Versailles addressed to the Governor, stressing that military matters were in the sole charge of Montcalm. It is probable that Montcalm was never informed of its contents.

By the middle of June the British were well up the St Lawrence. However, at Quebec the tidal rise was some nineteen feet, and expert navigation was required. Indeed the French had not expected the British to be able to manoeuvre men-of-war so far upstream. The British had what can only be described as a secret weapon in the person of one Captain James Cook, later to become the most celebrated navigator of his age. But there were also seasoned masters, such as Mr Killick of the *Goodwill*, whose opinion of the 'traverse', supposedly the most treacherous stretch of the river, was that there were 'a thousand places in the Thames fifty times more hazardous'.

Quebec is 700 miles from the Atlantic Ocean, but is the first major town on the St Lawrence River. It sits on high ground on the north bank of the river overlooking a natural basin to the east. At the eastern end of the basin is the Isle of Orleans. On the north side, midway between two tributaries, the Charles River to the west and the Montmorency on the east, was the settlement of Beauport. This north bank was the obvious place for any invading force to land. Montcalm, accordingly, had reinforced it with men and fortifications, and had erected a bridge over the Charles River to allow his troops free movement in and out of Quebec. Wolfe's first camp was on the south-eastern side of the Isle of Orleans, and the first troops were disembarked there on 27 June. Saunders was not happy with the anchorage, however, especially following an attack by French fireships on the 28th (they were towed out of course by British seamen with grappling hooks: 'Damn me, Jack, dids't thou ever take hell in tow before?'). He wanted to anchor in the basin. In order to do this it was necessary, at least, to command the heights on the south bank of the river at Point Levis. Wolfe sent in Monckton with a substantial force and the Point was taken with minimal effort. A battery was set up and Quebec began to feel its destructive power immediately. Saunders re-anchored his fleet.

In mid-July Wolfe moved his camp to the north bank, to the east of the Montmorency Falls (100 ft higher than Niagara). This was in preparation for an attack on Montcalm's positions.

This attack, carried out on 31 July, was a shambles. A clear, hot morning gave way by late afternoon to a ferocious storm. Wolfe reckoned his casualties at 210 killed and 230 wounded, though these were probably overestimates. Wolfe visited all the wounded.

On 5 August Wolfe sent Murray upriver in order to gather information and spread a little chaos in the French supply lines. He also wanted to know how Amherst's campaign was going. Murray returned some three weeks later, having destroyed a French supply depot, having been repulsed in an attempted landing twenty miles upstream, and with no news of Amherst. His long absence without communication had frustrated Wolfe: 'Murray, by his long stay above and by detaining all our boats, is actually master of the operations – or rather puts an entire stop to them,' he wrote to Monckton on 22 August. The relative fruitlessness of the expedition made Wolfe despondent. He wrote home of 'such a choice of difficulties' in determinining how best to proceed. He began to devastate the surrounding countryside, as he had promised he would: in February he had written that if he found Quebec 'not likely to fall' then he would 'destroy the harvest, houses and cattle both above and below'.

At the end of August Wolfe's already frail health deteriorated. There has been much speculation over the years as to the nature of his sickness during the siege of Quebec. He was certainly very ill, and often in considerable pain. Early in the campaign a subordinate officer's physical constitution had been called into question, and Wolfe had responded sharply: 'Don't talk to me of constitution. He has spirits, and spirits will carry a man through anything.' On 9 September he wrote what was to be his final despatch, to the Earl of Holderness, one of Pitt's advisers: 'I am so far recovered as to do business, but my constitution is entirely ruined.' Spirits would have to see him through. To his medical orderly at the end of August he had said: 'I know perfectly well you cannot cure my complaint, but pray make me up so that I may be without pain for a few days, and able to do my duty; that is all I want.' It is probable that, amongst other ailments, he was suffering from rheumatic fever.

While in this bout of severe illness, Wolfe instructed his brigadiers to confer on the best course of action, and they came unimously to the conclusion that battle could only be forced from the west. Wolfe accepted the recommendation at once.

James Wolfe

The Heights of Abraham and the St Lawrence River

137

The brigadiers, however, wanted to land troops much further upstream. It was Wolfe's tactical acuity that was required to see the possibility of splitting Montcalm's forces between those on the north bank of the river around Beauport and Quebec, and the large force that Bougainville commanded at Point de Trembles, some twenty miles to the west of the city.

On 1 September the British army began to make its way across the river to the south bank, and by the 4th it was ready to march upstream. Wolfe had hoped for reinforcements from Amherst, but there were none.

On the same day, the 4th, Wolfe fell seriously ill again, to such an extent that his survival was seriously in doubt. Had Wolfe died, Monckton would have assumed command. It is possible that Quebec would have finally surrendered to the brigadiers, but the operation would certainly have taken much longer, and had the winter arrived to threaten the British fleet, very much longer. Nor was Wolfe's presence merely that of a superior military intelligence. He was popular with his troops. This popularity had to do not so much with any warmth of personality as with the trust which he inspired in them. He took his soldiers' health very seriously, and their comfort. The contraction of venereal disease was discouraged (insofar as such a thing is possible) by stiff financial penalties (syphilis was more expensive than gonorrhea); uniforms were stripped of their more absurd particulars (high Prussian collars), and back-packs were to be carried 'as the Indians', high on the shoulders. Wolfe even went so far as to consider his soldiers as sentient beings and, in stark contrast to the way in which he treated his brigadiers, kept them apprised of the progress of the campaign. His troops were always highly trained, and were expected to fire three shots a minute. They knew they were good. And while Wolfe expected them to be good he was generous in rewarding merit. He had absolutely no patience with disobedience or indiscipline, and these in turn were treated ruthlessly.

As a man he was not especially lovable. He was cold and censorious. He once famously described the ladies of Glasgow as 'coarse, cold and cunning, for ever enquiring after men's circumstances'. He later added that they were 'cold to everything but a bagpipe; – I wrong them, there there is not one that does not melt away at the sound of an estate'. This suggests an envy which might have made him suspicious of those of higher social rank – such as his brigadiers.

Wolfe's pain kept him in bed on the 5th but on the following four days he scouted possible points for attack. He settled on the little gully across the river known as Anse du Foulon. This was less than a mile upstream from Quebec, and if he could get his forces to the top of the cliff in good order then the enemy would be split and, at last, he would have put his 'small number of good [soldiers]' in a position to fight Montcalm's 'great number of bad soldiers'. Throughout the campaign Wolfe had insisted that 'the army should be attacked in preference to the place'.

To say that this plan was audacious is to understate the case woefully. Montcalm clearly did not expect it. Indeed he was under the impression that Wolfe was concocting an elaborate bluff, and that his real target was again the north shore between the Charles and Montmorency Rivers. The French General even reinforced his artillery there.

The audacity lay not merely in the scaling of the Heights of Abraham, but also in the delicacy of timing required to land his troops at the most advantageous moment of the tide's ebb and flow. Secrecy and surprise were all, and Wolfe kept his plan very close to his chest. He did not inform his brigadiers of the particulars, but he did outline them to Colonel Burton of the Louisbourg Grenadiers: '. . . the fleet sails up the river a little higher, as if intending to land above upon the north shore, keeping a convenient distance for the boats and armed vessels to fall down to the Foulon; and we count (if no accident of weather or other prevents) to make a powerful effort at that spot about four in the morning of the 13th.'

In order to achieve this 'powerful effort' the navy was required to manoeuvre in astonishingly precise ways. Admiral Holmes, second in command to Saunders, wrote at the end of his life that this action was 'the most hazardous and difficult task I was ever engaged in'.

On the evening of 12 September Wolfe entrusted his Will to a young captain, John Jervis, later Lord St Vincent. He also handed to him a miniature of his fiancée, Katherine Lowther, to take back to her in the event of his death.

At 1.35 a.m. the first troops, some 1,800 Light Infantrymen, boarded the flat-bottomed boats that were then lowered into the river. The tide had turned and was beginning to ebb. The moon was in its final quarter, the weather was fine and the river flat. The tide pulled them down. At one point a French guard asked from the bank 'Qui vive?'. Captain Fraser of the 78th Highlanders responded with perfect aplomb 'La France. Vive le Roi.' A French supply convoy had been expected. This was clearly it.

Wolfe was with the first landing party. He looked up and turned to Colonel Howe of the Light Infantry: 'There seems scarcely a possibility of getting up, but you must do your endeavours.' It had begun to rain.

By daybreak there were 4,000 British troops on the plain at the top of the cliff. Montcalm would have to come out and fight. The British army stood four-square across his supply line. The French General on being shown the British remarked: 'Yes – I see them, where they ought not to be.' He sent a messenger for Bougainville and prepared to fight. At around 8 a.m he turned the guns of Quebec on the British army. Wolfe ordered his men to lie down.

The line of battle was very long, over half a mile. On the extreme left was Townshend, fending off snipers in the woods to the north. Then came Murray. Monckton held the centre. Wolfe posted himself on the right. By 9.30 Montcalm's army was drawn up opposite the British. It numbered about 7,000 troops of very varying efficiency. At 10 they began to advance towards the British line. They fired their first volley with little effect. The British held their fire. The French approached. Still Wolfe did not give the order to fire. Sixty yards. Fifty. When the French were forty yards away the British loosed a first volley. It devastated the French ranks. Wolfe had always insisted that fire should be held until one was sure of hitting one's target. This single volley, described by one military historian as 'the most perfect volley ever fired on a battlefield', effectively won the battle. Within fifteen minutes the French were in retreat. The rain stopped, the breeze fell, the sun came out.

Wolfe had been hit. Three times. The first two hits had injured him in the wrist and the groin. The third ripped open his chest. He called out 'Support me! Let not my brave soldiers see me drop. The day is ours. Keep it.'

There are a number of versions of Wolfe's death. He was removed from the heart of the fighting by a private soldier, James Henderson of the Louisbourg Volunteers, who wrote an account in a letter to his family: 'I open'd his breast and found his shirt full of blood at which he smiled and when he seen the distress I was in, "My Dear," said he, "Don't grieve for me I shall be happy in a few Minutes take care of Yourself as I see you are Wounded. But tell me O tell me how goes the Battle?"' At that point one or two officers appeared, and told him that the French were retreating. Now Wolfe insisted that the reserves be sent forward to the Charles River in order to cut off any retreat. He knew that many victories had been squandered by a reluctance to drive advantage home. Had his orders been obeyed, Quebec would more than likely have fallen that very day. As it was it took another week before the city finally capitulated and another year for the French to be finally defeated in Canada.

Wolfe had, however, won a great victory. His army lost fifty-eight officers and men killed, and 600 wounded. The French lost around 1,000 killed and wounded, including Montcalm himself, who died of his wounds the following day. Great battles are more than military. They have deeper resonances, and their 'greatness' is not always dependent on strategic genius. Wolfe's plan after three months was certainly audacious, its execution brilliant, but it was also desperate. The 'genius' was in the timing and in the circumstances. Great Britain had not had a military hero since Marlborough. The war had been dragging on inconclusively for three years. Wolfe was young and talented. And he had died.

Wolfe's body was embalmed and placed upon the *Royal William*, one of the longest serving ships in the history of the Royal Navy (commissioned in 1670 it was only broken up in 1813). The ship put in to Spithead on 16 November 1759. Wolfe was buried at St Alphege in Greenwich. His statue stands at the top of the hill in Greenwich Park looking down over the Royal Naval College. There is a monument at Westminster Abbey. In Quebec there is a stone column at the back of the Chateau Frontenac. On one side is the name WOLFE, on the other MONTCALM. There is a Latin inscription: 'Their valour gave them a common death, history a common glory, and posterity a common monument.' Heroes both.

Chapter Eight

Gallipoli

The high hopes most people had at the outbreak of the First World War that, in the famous saying, it would all be over by Christmas, were dashed within four months. After a large-scale and deceptively fast initial deployment of troops, the Western Front settled down into a massive and intractable stalemate. Across northern France and Belgium, the British and French faced the two Central Powers, Germany and Austria-Hungary, in a seemingly unending – and immovable – line of trenches. Alternative fronts had to be considered and the most discussed Eastern Front revolved around an attack on the Dardanelles, the forty-one-mile-long channel which, passing between the Gallipoli Peninsula and the Asiatic mainland, forms the gateway to the Sea of Marmara. The obvious prize of such a front was Constantinople, lying at the head of the Sea of Marmara and, from 31 October 1914, the capital of yet another country that had declared war on the Triple Entente of Britain, France and Russia. Turkey had been drawn into the war on the side of the Central Powers to counter the perceived threats from Greece and Russia and, apart from the obvious point of harming an enemy, the forcing of the Dardanelles seemed to promise other advantages – particularly to Winston Churchill, at that time the First Lord of the Admiralty. It was by no means an original plan, having been discussed and rejected as too difficult on several occasions. But this time it was felt that it could protect both the British in Egypt and the Suez Canal, the Russians in the Caucasus and their grain shipments from the Black Sea and deal a considerable blow to the stability of Austria-Hungary. Therefore, with the enthusiastic advocacy of Winston Churchill, a plan started to take shape in 1915 to force the heavily mined and defended waters of the Dardanelles.

Right from the very start of the Gallipoli campaign there was a fatal indecision about what the main strategy should be, how the objectives should be achieved – in fact, what the whole campaign amounted to. The Secretary of State for War, Lord Kitchener, sent the 29th Division, two battalions of Royal Marine Light Infantry and the French Corps Expéditionnaire d'Orient under General Albert d'Amade to the Aegean island of Lemnos. But both he and Churchill at first thought of them as a garrison rather than an invasion force, who would land on the Gallipoli Peninsula purely to clear out the Turkish forts after the navy had bombarded them. They did not envisage any substantial role for them.

There were three stages to the Turkish defence of the Dardanelles, the first comprising two permanent forts on the tip of the peninsula and rows of mines at the channel entrance. These were successfully neutralized on 19 February 1916, but the next stage of Turkish defences was a very different proposition. The much thicker wall of mines, protected by numerous coastal batteries, slowed up the Allies considerably and when they were forced, by mounting political pressure, to put sixteen ships into attack, they immediately lost three ships and three more were put out of action for a long time. This reversal shocked the Allies into realizing that there had to be a major military operation to secure the Turkish shoreline before the channel could be cleared. On 27 March, therefore, Churchill agreed to a combined operation and there was a sudden, frenetic burst of administrative activity as new troops were drafted in, new plans were laid and commanding officers appointed.

Field Marshal Otto von Sanders

Naturally, for such a major military reorganization, all the troops had to be assembled in one place and, as there was no room on Lemnos, the troops there were sent to Alexandria in Egypt, where they joined up with the Australian and New Zealand troops, known as the Anzacs, under the command of Lieutenant-General Birdwood. Apart from the inconvenience and clumsiness of all this going back and forward, the crucial disadvantage was that it lost the Allies all hope of surprising the Turks. On 25 March, the formidable German General Liman von Sanders was appointed commander of the Turkish 5th Army, responsible for defending the Gallipoli Peninsula, and he immediately started fortifying the peninsula's defences. His instincts were confirmed by numerous breaches of security while the Allied forces were still in Egypt which were relayed to him by the highly developed German Intelligence Service.

The combination of piecemeal strategy, carelessness and overconfidence cast an ominous shadow over the embarkation of what became known as the Mediterranean Expeditionary Force and when its Commander-in-Chief, General Sir Ian Hamilton, left Charing Cross on 13 March, he did so with some trepidation. 'This is going to be an unlucky show,' he is reported to have said, 'I kissed my wife through her veil.'

With the possibility of total surprise lost, Hamilton had to decide on a landing which would both fool the Turkish defences and allow the Allies to overcome the Turkish positions dominating the Dardanelles. The plan he decided on was essentially a good one. Its aim was to take the Kilid Bahr plateau, an expanse of high ground at the south-western end of the peninsula, and to do so, he proposed a main landing on five beaches at the tip of the peninsula, known as Cape Helles, by the 29th Division, backed up by the Anzacs' landing at Gaba Tepe, halfway up the peninsula on the Aegean coast. The Royal Navy Division was to make a feint attack at Bulair, on the north of the peninsula and, finally, the French were to land at Kum Kale, on the eastern side of the peninsula, to protect the rear of the Cape Helles landings. The 29th Division, after landing, would sweep up to the Achi Baba ridge. The Anzacs, similarly, would advance inland to the Mal Tepe ridge and both forces then would be in a position to dominate the Kilid Bahr plateau. Next stop Constantinople.

Although he did not know it, Hamilton had brilliantly anticipated Liman von Sanders's deployment of his forces. Most of the reinforcements he had rushed to Gallipoli were concentrated in the north, for an attack on Bulair, and around Kum Kale, for an attack from the Dardanelles. The south-western part of the peninsula was comparatively lightly defended and, thus, if the Allies could move fast, they might be able to make real progress. But for that Allied command would have to be flexible, resolute and, above all, prepared for the vigour with which the Turks would defend their country. Liman von Sanders's men were extremely mobile and committed to their task. They were not, as many of the Allies complacently expected, simply going to roll over.

This complacency was the first drawback Hamilton had to contend with. It was made far worse by the unfortunate appointment of General Aylmer Hunter Weston as commander of the 29th Division; 'Hunter-Bunter', as he was known, was something of a caricature, a Colonel Blimp figure of absurd self-importance and vanity. But, even worse, he was a simplistic and narrow-minded tactician who only cared about attacking in the most straightforward and unsubtle way. 'Casualties?' he was once heard to say, 'what do I care about casualties?' Hamilton could easily have counteracted his worst excesses but for some reason he was obsessed by the idea that a commander-in-chief shouldn't interfere directly in battle. Moreover, because of the very poor lines of communication, Hamilton was often in the dark about exact events and he was constantly aware that Lord Kitchener was very reluctant to send either fresh troops or, even more essentially, fresh ammunition to support what Kitchener thought fundamentally a secondary mission.

The Gallipoli campaign, therefore, was finely balanced right from its very outset – certainly far more of a close-run thing than any of the Allies anticipated. It lasted over eight months, but it turned on just a handful of brief moments, instances of retreat or advance, hesitancy and indecision, on the one hand, and determined, fearless leadership on the other – all of which were not recognized immediately for what they implied in the furious confusion of battle. It was only later that both sides understood what might have been. One such moment occurred almost instantly on the first day of the campaign, 25 April 1916, when the Anzac covering forces went in to land at Gaba Tepe before dawn.

It was not a good beginning. Instead of landing just north of Gaba Tepe, the Anzacs found themselves going ashore north of Hell Spit, mainly in a cove that came to be known as Anzac Cove. It's unclear whether they were taken that far by the current or by a midshipman correcting his position in the dark, but as they hit the beaches they knew things were pretty confused and that the cliffs in front of them were much steeper than they'd been led to expect. The worst were north of Ari Burnu, but Plugge's Plateau rising above Anzac Cove was pretty bad. The landing beach, as well, was only a few hundred yards rather than a mile long. Nevertheless, they all were so aware of the importance of speed that they set off immediately and by 6 a.m. about 4,000 Anzacs were ashore with not many more than 700 Turks to oppose them. The landing had obviously been a complete surprise and the forward parties marched blithely, if slightly uncomprehendingly, over the ridges and hills that soon would become amongst the most fiercely fought-over plots of land in history. Baby 700, The Nek, 400 Plateau, Battleship Hill – these were the names given to the crucial strips of land, the promontories and gentle hill slopes, that in this dizzying and pitiless terrain of plunging gorges and ravines would determine who held the superior position. And, on that early morning of 25 April, the Anzacs were occupying them all.

When the Turkish 9th Divisional Commander, Khalil Sami Bey, heard that the Anzacs had landed at Gaba Tepe, he thought that it was only a feint to cover the real landings at Bulair. But the Commander of the 19th Division, Mustafa Kemal Bey – the future Atatürk – also heard the news at the same time and he interpreted it very differently. He was ordered to send one of his battalions, but taking matters into his own hands, he knew that only his whole division would be enough and he set off straight away to the heights above Gaba Tepe. As he arrived, he saw Turks fleeing towards him from Battleship Hill. Despite their pleading that they would be overwhelmed, he ordered them to turn and lie down, facing the Anzacs with their bayonets fixed. His bluff worked and, instead of attacking them, the Anzacs lay down too and lost the momentum that they never recovered.

The Turks had time to rush further reinforcements to Gaba Tepe and, although by 2 p.m. on 25 April the Anzacs had landed 12,000 men to face 4,000 Turks, the pendulum had swung in the opposite direction. There was utter confusion in Anzac Cove, with barely any room to accommodate new arrivals or take out casualties, and shrapnel had started pounding the beach. All the units were hopelessly mixed up and the Turks had started counter-attacking. By 5 p.m. the Anzacs were clinging on grimly and praying for the day to end. Baby 700 alone changed hands five times, defence and attack was equally uncoordinated, the Anzacs had taken up uniformly bad positions and the Turks fought with the most unquenchable ardour. As Kemal Bey said, 'Everybody hurled himself on the enemy to kill and to die. This was no ordinary attack. Everybody in this attack was eager to succeed or go forward with the determination to die.' All that was clear, as night started to fall, was that the Anzacs were equally determined not to be driven into the sea.

The landings on the five beaches at Cape Helles by the British 29th Division took place later than the Anzac landings and were preceded by a massive naval bombardment. Both landings on the flank, on Y beach on the Aegean coast and S beach on the Dardanelles side, caught the Turks completely by surprise and passed off with very few casualties. The problem was that, once ashore, the British had been ordered to wait for the main forces coming up from the south and given no alternative courses of action if they did not arrive. Therefore, even though the forces who landed at Y beach were stronger than all the Turkish troops between Achi Baba, the poppy-covered ridge near them, and Cape Helles, they didn't set off to link up with the other beaches but merely dug in and waited. The troops at S beach did the same and their wait would not have been a long one if the story in the south had all been the same as at X beach, the smallest of the main landings. A certain Major Cuthbert Lucas has passed down the incredible picture of him landing there on a beautifully sunny morning, a bag in one hand, his coat over his arm and a helpful sailor assisting him down the plank so that his boots would not get wet. The British got ashore on X beach as if they were on a boating trip or checking in to a hotel.

But on W and V beaches the story was a very different one. They were both smooth, gently sloping expanses of sand surrounded by cliffs – the perfect Mediterranean holiday beach – and thus ideal both for landing and for defence. The Turks had covered them with barbed wire and ringed the cliffs with machine-guns and, despite the intensity of the naval bombardment, none of the Turkish positions was dislodged. They simply retreated during the worst part of the bombing and then returned to their emplacements. So, when the Lancashire Fusiliers approached the shore in tow boats, they couldn't have presented an easier target. Men were picked off while they were still in the boats, as they dropped into the water, weighed down by their guns and equipment, as they scrambled onto the beach and came up against the first rows of barbed wire. Their guns seized up in the sea water and the fine sand of the beach, and there was nowhere to hide – they could only drive on towards the cliffs. Eleven officers and 350 men were killed instantly on landing but, by great determination and courage, they managed to force their way up the cliffs.

On V beach to the east, even that amount of progress was impossible. A collier called the *River Clyde* was run ashore and the 2,000 men inside were meant to run down the specially built gangways over a bridge of light vessels and onto the beach. The minute they emerged, they were caught in a murderous hail of fire, the gangways soon becoming thronged with dead bodies, while behind them more men marched forward to their death. The tow boats bringing in the rest of the invasion force were riddled with incendiary shells and machine-gun fire, the soldiers either being shot, drowned, suffocated by the weight of dead bodies crushing them or burnt to death. The few men that made it to the beach were held up by barbed wire and the only thing that prevented the entire force being wiped out was a small bank of sand, between five and eight feet high, which was ten yards in from the water's edge. The survivors desperately flung themselves behind this bank while the sea, stained black with blood, filled up with piles of dead bodies and boats drifting aimlessly with their mutilated cargo.

It was a terrible scene and even now it is profoundly shocking to think that Hunter Weston, who was stationed on a warship off W beach, could have relied on hopelessly misleading information and ordered the landing to continue. To land more men was quite clearly to send them to their deaths and it was only when Hamilton saw personally what was happening that the landing was halted. But wave after wave of men were killed and, although Hamilton recognized immediately that they should press home their advantage on the flanks, he did no more than politely suggest this to Hunter Weston, who peremptorily rufused.

The night of 25 April 1916 was freezing cold and wet and while darkness brought some respite, it spelled out to the majority of the Mediterranean Expeditionary Force how desperate their position was. The Anzacs were barely hanging on and, in anticipation of a fierce counter-attack the next morning, their divisional commanders did actually consider evacuation. But they changed their minds by the time Hamilton's order to stay put reached them with its famous postscript: 'You have got through the difficult business, now you have only to dig, dig, dig until you are safe.'

All through the night and over the following days, the Allied casualties suffered agonies. Allied command had prepared for only 3,000 casualties in all for the campaign's first phase, but on 25 April alone there were 5,000. The hospital ships and the transports converted into auxiliary hospitals were full by early evening and it was a common sight to see boats loaded down with wounded being shunted from one transport to another. Once on board, the chronic lack of doctors, the fact that the transports couldn't leave for the base hospitals in case the troops had to be re-embarked and that, when they could leave, they made the longer journey to Alexandria rather than Lemnos – all this incompetence meant that most wounds became putrified and developed gangrene, and the general suffering was increased enormously.

Such an opening to the campaign must have had a huge effect on morale and perhaps accounts for the events of the decisive second day. For, despite having suffered much greater losses than expected, the Allies had 20,000 troops on Gallipoli on 26 April as opposed to 6,300 Turks, and the entire Turkish resistance south of Achi Baba had collapsed. But instead of ordering his men to advance, Hunter Weston had them dig in and prepare for an attack. 'There will be no retiring,' he commanded. 'Every man will die at his post rather than retire.' The Turks, therefore, were given time to rush reinforcements south and by the time the British were ready to move on 28 April, Hunter Weston had ensured that his men would die, not at their posts, but on the brutally exposed spurs leading up to Achi Baba. Over the next few weeks, thousands of troops from both sides were slaughtered in some of the most ferocious warfare in the First World War.

Perhaps the most terrible aspect of the fighting was its predictability. Each morning would dawn with the same beautiful, still Mediterranean sunlight. At the appointed hour a murderous bombardment on the Turkish trenches would start up, which promised much but achieved so little that when the Allies climbed out of their trenches they would be mown down by the same devastating machine-gun fire. A trench here or there might change hands, but then the Turks would counter-attack and, by evening, the Allies would be clinging on with the last reserves of strength. Between 6 and 8 May, in what is known as the Second Battle of Krithia, the Allies suffered 6,000 casualties for a gain of only 600 yards. There were so many acts of heroism in those terrible days that it is hard to single out any individual ones, but the Australian advance up Krithia Spur burnt itself into the memory of all who witnessed it. As one British major who saw it said, 'The enemy's shelling was shifted onto them in one great concentration of hell. The machine-guns bellowed and poured on them sheets of flame and of ragged death, buried them . . . But what of it? Why, nothing! They were as devils from a hell bigger and hotter. Nothing could stop them . . . They were not men, but gods, demons infuriated. We saw them fall by the score . . . Not for one breath did the great line waver or break. On and on it went, up and on, as steady and proud as if on parade. A seasoned officer watching choked with his own admiration. Our men tore off their helmets and waved them, and poured cheer after cheer after those wonderful Anzacs.'

Gallipoli has become, in many ways, synonymous with Anzac heroism. At Gaba Tepe, it was their ferocious defence, rather than official indecision, that repelled the Turks and created a deadlock.

In the first six days they suffered 6,554 casualties and inflicted over 14,000 and, after a final near suicide charge on 1 May, they dug themselves in to create the most unique and tenacious foothold in history. Their domain was no more than a mile and a half long from north to south, with the front line a mere 1,000 yards from the sea at its furthest point inland, and it was shelled and shot up by rifle fire without pause both day and night. As spring gave way to a mercilessly hot summer, the cramped quarters and piles of dead bodies became a virulent breeding ground for disease. Swarms of green flies – or 'corpse flies', as they were known – hovered over the dead and dysenteric diarrhoea swept through the ranks, wiping out as many men as those fighting. By August, the Anzacs were losing as many as 10 per cent of their numbers a week, which doesn't count the walking skeletons who stayed at their post.

For nothing could dismay them. They were all determined to carry on and the incredible story of a private who had carried bullets in his thigh, his diaphragm, liver and side, a compound fracture of the arm and dysentery for five months before finally, and extremely apologetically, consulting a doctor, bears witness to their prodigious courage. They feared nothing, neither authority nor the enemy and, in fact, after the Armistice of 24 May, an astonishing camaraderie developed between the rank and file of both sides. The Anzacs would throw tins of bully-beef into the Turkish trenches only yards away and, once, cigarettes came back with the note, 'Prenez avec plaisir a notre heros ennemis.'

If Allied leadership had lived up to the Anzacs' example, then Gallipoli would have been won. As it was, the sacrifices made by so many heroes at Gallipoli has gone down in history and shaped the proud traditions of Australia and New Zealand. One need only quote the charge of the Australian 3rd Light Horse Brigade on 7 August to understand why.

As part of a final push, the Allies had made a fresh landing at Suvla Bay, north of Gaba Tepe, on 6 August, which was meant to link up with the Anzacs breaking out to the north of their lines and then, in tandem, swing round to attack the Turks in the rear. As a distraction, the Anzacs mounted an incredible attack on the strongest part of the Turkish line at the ridge known as Lone Pine, which, against all the odds, was a success. But the flanking troops needed all support possible, so it was decided that at 4.30 a.m. on 7 August the 3rd Light Horse Brigade would charge at point-blank range across a ridge that was barely wide enough for 150 men to advance at a time. The Light Horsemen did not care that they were heading straight into

Heroes

a wall of machine-gun fire. They were consumed with youthful enthusiasm, a hunger for great deeds and pride at the Lone Pine victory. Not for a minute did they doubt that they would burst through the trenches and clear out the other side to open country.

At 4 a.m., therefore, a thunderous bombardment began and rained down on the Turkish trenches for twenty-three minutes. Suddenly it stopped. Silence fell and for seven minutes nothing moved but clouds of dust. Promptly at 4.30 a.m., the Light Horsemen leapt from the trenches and charged forward in piercing sunlight. The first wave was mown down in seconds. Another followed, then another, then another and by 4.45 the ground was totally covered with dead and wounded. Out of the 600 who charged so gallantly on that fateful morning, 372 were killed or wounded. Their heroic legacy will never be forgotten.

The Battle of Cambrai 1917

This was the scene of the world's first massed tank attack. On 20 December, the 434 vehicles of Brigadier-General Elles's Tank Corps, supported by an inadequate number of infantry and 40,000 cavalry, rolled over the Hindenburg Line west of Cambrai in an attempt to break the cycle of trench warfare. By mid-morning they had routed the Germans on a six-mile front, and Cambrai was open for the taking. Indecisive leadership resulted in the cavalry failing to capitalize on the break-through. By 30 November, many tanks had broken down; the Germans counter-attacked with a hail of poison gas shells, and the British had to withdraw from the salient they had created. They suffered 40,000 killed and wounded; the Germans lost a similar number. A year later, Allied success in the Cambrai area, and the influx of American forces, began the startling series of victories that led to the German capitulation.

Chapter Nine

Guardians of the Bridge

Traditionally, Rome was founded in 753 BC by Romulus and ruled by a monarchy for nearly 250 years. During the time of the kings, the tiny settlement of a few villages overlooking the Tiber and inhabited by shepherds and farmers grew into a genuine fortified city, complete with defensive ramparts, fine public buildings and temples.

For the first 150 years monarchy served Rome well, expanding its dominions by conquest and instituting a political system where decisions were made jointly by the king, the Senate, an assembly of one hundred aristocrats and the general populace. But around 600 BC, at the end of Ancus Martius's reign, power struggles began to break out with the arrival of the foreigner Lucius Tarquinius Priscus and his Etruscan wife, Tanaquil.

A formidably ambitious couple, they made sure that Lucius Tarquinius Priscus was indispensable to Ancus and he was soon appointed adviser in foreign, domestic and palace affairs and made guardian to Ancus's two sons. At Ancus's death, Lucius Tarquinius Priscus, for the first time, called for an election and, thanks to his great eloquence, he was elected king in place of Ancus's son. He then secured his position by appointing one hundred new senators loyal to him, who not only sanctioned his thirty-eight-year-long reign but also allowed Tanaquil to choose his successor. Instead of Ancus's son, the next king of Rome was Servius Tullius, who had been a slave in the palace before a miraculous event led Tanaquil to bring him up as part of the royal family. When he was young, Servius had fallen asleep and a crown of flames had appeared around his head. In consternation, everyone in the palace, including the king and his wife, had hurried to see this strange phenomenon. The majority felt that Servius should be woken up, but Tanaquil alone was convinced that they should leave him to wake up naturally and only then would he be unharmed. Sure enough, Servius soon woke up and the flames vanished, convincing everyone that he was destined for a great future. He married Lucius Tarquinius Priscus's daughter and, when Priscus was assassinated on the orders of Ancus's embittered sons, Tanaquil made sure that Servius took over.

Servius's mild and honourable reign of forty-four years was, for many people, the last true expression of kingship in Rome and it is suggested that he wanted to hand over rule to the Senate and transform Rome into a republic, since he felt that there was nothing more a king could do for the common good of Rome. He waged a successful war against the Veii and other neighbouring Etruscan cities, which added to Rome's sphere of influence and, out of the land he had won, he gave a great part to the common people.

Unfortunately, this only added to the number of enemies ranged against him in Rome. Ancus's sons, of course, were mortally insulted by his reign, but their enmity was nothing compared to that of Lucius Tarquinius – soon to be known as Lucius Tarquinius Superbus, or Tarquin the Proud – who was a son of Lucius Tarquinius Priscus. In an unholy echo of his parents' marriage, Lucius's sense of injustice was soon fanned by the rapacious ambition of an Etruscan princess named Tullia. The fact that Lucius was married to Tullia's sister and Tullia to Lucius's brother did not strike them as a major obstacle. They simply killed their respective spouses and married each other, and Tullia set to work immediately, goading her new husband to take over the throne. He solicited support from the patrician families who had been put out by Servius's grant of land to the common people, he offered the younger men money and, when the moment was right, he forced his way into the Forum and took his place on the king's throne in the Senate. While he was delivering a brutal attack on Servius's background and ability to rule, Servius marched in to the Senate. But Lucius gave him no time to speak, physically throwing the older man out and then having his assassins murder him and leave his body in the street. Tullia, typically, was the first to enter the Senate and hail Lucius as the king and then, as she was hurrying home to escape the crowds who had filled the Forum, her charioteer pointed out Servius's body lying in the street in front of them. She paused for a moment and then ordered her charioteer to drive on, straight over the corpse. Blood spurted all over the carriage and Tullia herself and, for a long while afterwards, that street was known as the Street of Crime.

Having seized power in such a way in 532, Lucius Tarquinius Superbus's reign could never have been anything other than a time of intimidation and cruelty. 'Since they won't love me, let them fear me' was his motto. Servius was denied a decent burial and the power of the Senate was systematically broken down, both by the drafting of craven new senators who would do anything Lucius wished and by a campaign of open hostility against all of Rome's most important and capable men. Anyone who incurred Lucius's displeasure by having a mind of their own or a sense of civic justice was exiled or executed and those who had any sort of wealth were condemned on trumped-up charges and their property confiscated.

Twenty-three years of terror passed in which the only hope for those who cared for liberty was to become invisible. No one pursued this course with more subtlety and courage than the king's nephew, Lucius Junius, who watched in silent horror as his brother and other brave men were put to death. Not only did he not react, he gave such a convincing impression of being a simpleton that he became known as 'Brutus' – the dullard – and, passing as an innocuous and simple-minded soul, he bided his time at the heart of Lucius's court.

Devastating as it was for the inhabitants of Rome, the proud king's ruthlessness made him a formidable opponent for Rome's neighbours. He overcame many towns, instituted an enormous programme of public building and, in the last campaign of his reign, he laid siege to the Rutulian town of Ardea. It was a drawn-out siege which gave the officers plenty of time to entertain themselves and at one dinner they were all sitting around, reciting the merits of their wives. An officer called Collatinus suggested that they ride back to Rome and judge their wives' characters by seeing what they were doing at such a late hour. All the princes' wives were enjoying themselves at a party in the palace but Collatinus's wife, Lucretia, was still working hard, spinning with her maids by lamplight. She was, therefore, unanimously voted the most virtuous but Collatinus gained only sorrow from his wife's excellence. For Sextus, another of the king's sons, decided that he must possess Lucretia and a week later he brutally raped her at swordpoint.

Lucretia immediately called her father and her husband, who came to the house with Brutus, to tell them what had happened and, although they instantly believed her and swore that she was in no way to blame, nonetheless she committed suicide out of shame. At that moment Brutus revealed his true character.

'By this girl's blood – none more chaste till a tyrant wronged her – ', Brutus proclaimed, 'and by the gods I swear that with sword and fire, and whatever else can lend strength to my arm, I will pursue Lucius Tarquinius the Proud, his wicked wife and all his children and never again

will I let them or any other man be king of Rome.'
Lucretia's body was taken outside and displayed, and this
crime crystallized all the revulsion that Lucius's reign had
provoked. Brutus was enthusiastically hailed as Rome's
liberator, the troops at Ardea rallied to his side and the king
was barred from the city, fleeing instead in exile to Caere in
Etruria. Brutus and Collatinus were elected by the Senate as
Rome's first consuls and the Roman people swore an oath
that they would allow no one to be king or threaten Rome's
liberties.

All too soon, this oath was put to the test. Lucius
Tarquinius went round the Etruscan towns trying to enlist
support for his reinstatement and he found plenty of kings
ready to listen to his arguments. After all, he was of
Etruscan blood like them, republicanism might threaten
their rule if it became popular throughout Italy and he
could promise them substantial rewards. The Veii and
Tarquinii responded first and, in a massive battle, the
Romans managed just to defeat them, but only after Brutus
and Arruns, one of Tarquinius's sons, had killed each other.
Far more alarming was the decision of Lars Porsena, the
king of Clusium, to take up Lucius Tarquinius's cause. He
was the most powerful of all the Etruscans and Clusium the
finest of all the well-fortified Etruscan cities to the north of
Rome, which had grown wealthy from their many
industries and extensive trade with Greece and the Middle
East. As he gathered together his vast army, the Romans
panicked, rushing within the city walls and leaving only
their army outside. The army itself was racked with fear
and, when Lars Porsena advanced towards the Janiculum,
the last hill before Rome's walls, it lost all control and
started fleeing in confusion towards the wooden bridge
which was the most vulnerable point in Rome's defences. It
was every man for himself as they ran chaotically down the
hill and, if it had not been for the soldier guarding the

bridge, Lars Porsena's forces would have entered Rome straight away. One man alone, Publius Horatius Cocles, prevented the inevitable.

Like Brutus, Publius Horatius Cocles was a fearless defender of Rome's freedom who bided his time, quite content to remain in the background until he was most needed. As he saw his fellow soldiers break ranks and flee in disorder, he knew his time had come. Shouting at the top of his voice, he stopped their flight and stated that if they did not make a stand, soon the Palatine and the Capitol would be overwhelmed by Etruscans. They must not be allowed over the bridge. He would defend it, but the soldiers must cross to the other side and destroy it. He would give them all the time they needed. For a moment, everyone was too dumbfounded to take in what he proposed. But then they set to work and two Romans of equal courage, Spurius Lartius and Titus Herminius, volunteered to stand by Horatius. Standing shoulder to shoulder, they bestrode the bridge and, as the Etruscans hurled themselves at them, they did not give an inch. They took the Etruscan spears on their shields and drove their swords through any who came within reach. It was brutal, frenzied fighting. The Etruscan dead piled up at their feet, but still they kept on coming. Horatius's right-hand men soon could take no more and retreated but Horatius knew that he must gain more time for the bridge to be destroyed. So he stayed and, incredibly, started mocking the Etruscans, calling them slaves of tyrants who had no pride in themselves, no honour, only a creeping servility that saw them want to rob others of their freedom. He challenged the Etruscans one by one to fight him in single combat and, out of amazement and shame, they were momentarily paralysed, none of them knowing how to respond to this stubborn, heroic man. Lars Porsena quickly brought them to their senses and they started throwing their spears and advancing on Horatius in one mass. They would have forced their way past him by sheer weight of numbers but just at that moment the bridge crashed into the river. With a prayer to Father Tiber, Horatius followed it in full armour and, even though there was a fierce current, he swam across to the other side. Amazingly, his courage alone had kept the Etruscans out of the city and even though Lars Porsena laid siege to Rome, there were so many who would give up their lives after Horatius's example that he was forced eventually to lift the siege. In recognition of his bravery, the Senate erected a statue to Horatius and gave him as much land as he could plough in a day.

Twenty-five years later, the Greek city states were in much the same position as Rome when Brutus expelled Lucius Tarquinius Priscus, the only difference being one of scale. From the eighth century BC, the Greek world had been expanding both westwards, to Italy and Sicily, and east-wards towards Ionia, the west coast of modern Turkey, sending out a steady stream of colonists who set up cities in every way identical to their Greek parents. In the west, this expansion went unchecked and Carthage, the major non-Greek power, for the most part left the Greek cities in Italy and Sicily alone. But in the east, the Greek colonies came up against the imposing and domineering presence of the Persian Empire, whose lands stretched from Egypt throughout Ancient Mesopotamia to the edge of the Russian steppe.

At the start of the sixth century BC, the Ionian colonies revolted against the Persians and in retaliation against Athenian and Spartan support for the uprising, Darius invaded Greece. In 490 BC, Darius's massive army was famously defeated at the Battle of Marathon and it was clear that it was only a matter of time before the Persians once again moved up the west Mediterranean coast looking for revenge. The death of Darius and a revolt in Egypt meant that, in fact, the Greeks were given ten years' grace, but in 481 BC, Darius's son, Xerxes, began making preparations for a fresh invasion and he sent envoys to all the Greek city states demanding that, as a sign of submission to his rule, they send back earth and water. The response was varied. The city states did not tend to think of themselves as a unified nation and, obviously, the further east they were, the more likely they were to compromise their liberty by accepting Persian rule – perhaps hoping that actual inter- ference would be minimal. But the reaction of Athens and Sparta was an unequivocal. They rejected Xerxes's presumption out of hand, the Spartans throwing his envoys into a well, telling them that if they wanted earth and water, they could find them at the bottom.

At a time when armies were comparatively large in proportion to their country's population, Xerxes's army was a prodigy that had never been seen before. Every corner of the Empire sent troops and ships. Indians, Medes, Babylonians, Egyptians, Bactrians, Libyans, Ethiopians, Syrians, Phrygians, Thracians – the list is endless, and they were backed up by an incredible supply network. In order to cross the Hellespont, Xerxes joined over 700 ships, which were anchored and tied to the land. Across their decks planks were laid, then a layer of brushwood and, finally, a layer of beaten earth, so that his army could march across the sea for all the world as if they were strolling down a modern highway. Herodotus's statistics and his claim that it took seven full days for Xerxes's army to pass before him in review are obvious exaggerations but they illustrate not simply poetic licence but the awesome effect the army produced on all who saw it. One witness is supposed to have asked in desperation why a god had transformed himself into Xerxes in order to lead the whole world's population to devastate Greece. The god could perfectly well have destroyed Greece without going to so much trouble. Xerxes himself could not imagine that anyone would dare to fight his army and when Demaratus, an exiled Spartan travelling with his army, told him that the Spartans would never accept slavery nor retreat in battle, however appalling the odds, Xerxes thought it so ridiculous that he burst out laughing and dismissed Demaratus good-humouredly.

Resistance, nonetheless, was fully under way, with the Athenians, under Themistocles, taking command at sea and the Spartans, under Leonidas, leading the troops on land. Both city states had consulted the Delphic Oracle about their chances and what course of action they should take. The advice given them was grim and perplexing – in Sparta's case they were told that either their city would be sacked or their king killed, and Athens was told that only the 'wooden wall' would not fall. By an inspired piece of interpretation, Themistocles decided that the 'wooden wall' must refer to Athens's navy, rather than its city walls, and so he led the Greek fleet to Artemisium, a strip of coast facing the northernmost tip of the island of Euboea, to await the arrival of the enormous Persian fleet which was steadily approaching, hugging the Mediterranean coast. Leonidas, the king of Sparta whose family could trace their line back to Hercules, decided that if he must sacrifice his life, then that would be a small price to pay for the safety of his city and so he set about deciding the best place to resist the Persian Army.

At first, 10,000 Greeks set out to hold Tempe, the pass between Mount Olympus and Mount Ossa which leads from lower Macedonia to Thessaly. But when it was dis-covered that there was another pass leading into Thessaly, which Xerxes did, in fact, take, the Greeks abandoned their position and settled on the pass of Thermopylae near Trachis in the land of the Malians as the breach which they would hold. A narrow road at most fifty feet wide, with, on one side, rugged and impassable cliffs and, on the other, a sheer drop to the sea, Thermopylae seemed to suit the Greeks perfectly. It had been used by the Phoenicians before to keep back the Thessalians and the Greeks set about rebuilding the wall which they had built across it.

It so happened that the Olympic festival took place at just the time the Greeks decided to hold Thermopylae, so the city states only sent advance parties to the pass, the Spartans leading the way as an example to the others, with the intention of sending the rest of their troops when the festival had finished. Three hundred heavily-armed Spartan infantry and similarly sized contingents from Arcadia, Boeotia and Corinth took up position in a state of confident but fairly relaxed readiness. This was partly a reflection of the innate confidence of these fierce warriors. No matter how powerful the Persian armies, they knew that Xerxes was not immortal and thus, like any human, susceptible to misfortune at some time or another. But their confidence also sprang from the conviction that time was on their side and the Persians would not attack before the Olympic festival was over and the main armies had arrived.

The general confidence of the Greeks rose even more when the Persian navy lost 400 ships in terrible storm at sea. But confidence turned to consternation when the Persian army reached Thermopylae while the Olympic festival was still in progress and, at a hastily called conference, the Peloponnesians urged that the army should fall back to the Isthmus of Corinth, even if that meant giving up all the city states between there and Trachis, including Athens, to the Persians. Leonidas wouldn't hear of it. He sent an appeal for more troops but, in the meantime, ordered the men to prepare for battle and none did so with more nonchalance and precision than the Spartans. Of all the Greeks, theirs was the most experienced army and Sparta itself, with its 5,000 warrior of the officer class and 5,000 shepherds, was less a country with a strong army than a city state permanently in arms. The 300, therefore, matter-of-factly set about exercising and the famous saying of a certain Dieneces sums up their implacable mood. A local had rushed up to tell him that the Persian archers were so numerous that when they fired, their arrows blotted out the sun. 'This is pleasant news that the stranger from Trachis brings us,' he laconically replied. 'If the Persians hide the sun, we shall have our battle in the shade.'

When a Persian spy saw the Spartans, he could hardly believe what he had to report to Xerxes, that so few men were actually going to fight such an awesome force. Xerxes was convinced that they were actually just waiting for the right moment to escape and so delayed his attack for four days. But on the fifth day, when they hadn't moved, he furiously ordered his Median and Cissian troops to attack and take them alive. They charged, but in such a confined space and against the longer spears of the Greeks, not only could they not capture anybody, they could hardly defend themselves. Rank after rank of infantry fell and, although they were immediately replaced, Xerxes soon realized that the size of an army is no compensation for the lack of real soldiers. He therefore sent in the finest Persian troops, the hand-picked Ten Thousand, known as the King's Immortals, under Hydarnes but they too foundered against the unbreakable wall of Greek spears. The Spartans repeatedly tricked the Persians with their manoeuvres, pretending, for instance, to retreat and turning their backs, only to wheel in perfect formation and inflict terrible casualties on the overconfident and gullible Persians. All day long the fighting raged and by nightfall the Persians had made no progress and the Greeks had suffered few losses. The next day, the Persians attacked again after sunrise but twelve hours later only the ranks of their dead had swelled and Thermopylae was no closer to being taken.

Heroes

The deadlock would have continued indefinitely if a certain Malian named Ephialtes had not been driven by the hope of a large reward to tell Xerxes of a path that led along the ridge of the mountains overlooking Thermopylae. Apparently this path was a matter of local knowledge but no one had told the Greeks about it and, although they had stationed the Phoenicians on higher ground, they had no one guarding against a full flanking movement. Xerxes was naturally delighted and, at dusk, sent Hydarnes and the Immortals along the path. By dawn, they were at the summit of the ridge where the Phoenicians were on guard and, taking them by surprise, the Immortals brushed past them and outflanked the Greeks with all 10,000 of their number intact.

By daybreak the Greeks were in no doubt of their impending destruction and, at another conference, their army split up, with the majority returning to their respective cities. They went with Leonidas's blessing, since he didn't want them to stay if their hearts weren't fully committed, but the thought that he and his 300 might retreat as well simply did not arise. Spartan honour forbade them to retreat in battle – this was the code of honour they had grown up in and so this was the code of honour they were going to die by. At their side stood the Thespian and Theban contingents.

On the last day of Thermopylae, Xerxes poured a libation to the rising sun and then, relishing his imminent victory, he waited until it was climbing in the sky before ordering the final attack. Knowing that they had nothing to lose, the Greeks moved out from behind the wall into a wider part of the pass and furiously beat back the Persians. One line of Persians after another fell on Greek spears or were forced off the road into the sea, their bodies piling up and trampled upon by the fresh waves of infantry driven on by the whips of their commanders. So desperately did the

Greeks fight that all their spears were broken and they fought on with their swords. Leonidas himself was killed in the thick of the fighting and a titanic struggle broke out for his body, four times in succession the Greeks winning it back from the Persians. Then the terrible moment arrived when Hydarnes and his men pressed in on them from the rear. The Greeks retreated to the narrowest part of the pass behind the wall and took their last stand packed together in one mass on a small and gently sloping hill. None of the Persians could dislodge them with their swords but such a small, compact body was too easy a target for missiles and so, finally, the Persian spearmen and archers killed the last of the Greeks. The Battle of Thermopylae was over and the Persians free to pass through.

The effect of Leonidas's and the Greeks' heroism were tremendous. They did not stop Xerxes's advance. The Greek naval victory at Salamis and military victory at Plataea achieved that. But they set a standard for Greek resistance that the Persians could never match, for fear and power alone could never instill in men's hearts the burning love of liberty that inspired the guardians of Thermopylae. It is the least they deserve that history has never forgotten their courage and the inscription set up as a memorial to them. 'Go tell the Spartans, you who read,' it said. 'We took their orders, and are dead.'

Chapter Ten

John Paul Jones

The first American Navy, consisting of two armed merchant ships, two armed brigantines, or brigs, and one armed sloop, was created by Act of the Second Continental Congress on 13 October 1775. Maryland's delegate to the Congress, Samuel Chase, summed up the general scepticism this undertaking provoked when he called it 'the maddest idea in the world'. The most thorough-going sceptics, who generally came from non-mercantile areas inland of the American coast, questioned whether there was any point in the Colonies going to great expense to become a sea power. The vast body of opinion, however, did not doubt that the Colonies desperately needed a navy. They just didn't think it stood a chance.

David and Goliath is the obvious comparison, but even that doesn't come close to describing the disparity between the American and British – or Royal – Navies. Britannia, at this stage, truly did rule the waves. In the 1770s, the Royal Navy had one hundred ships-of-the-line – that is, warships with over sixty guns. The Netherlands had only eleven ships-of-the-line. The Colonies had none. Their largest warship, the 350 ton *Alfred*, had only thirty guns, and quite apart from the number of guns, the American Navy had only five ships in all – with thirteen frigates under construction.

The Royal Navy, of course, had the problem of distance to contend with. It had to transport supplies all the way across the Atlantic and it had to perform the difficult task of simultaneously protecting these convoys and blockading

Admiral John Paul Jones

the whole of the American coast. Its commanders
quarrelled amongst themselves, organization was slipshod.
sailors deserted and diseases and the hostility of the French
and Spanish Navies were constant threats. But even after
taking these disadvantages into consideration, the
American Navy, at its creation, still only had less than a
third of the ships and less than a quarter of the guns that the
Royal Navy could muster in American waters. Not surpris-
ingly, therefore, the chance of serving in the American
Navy was not something that many people leapt at.

For some people, joining up was as good as committing
suicide. Members of the Patriot Party, for instance, refused
commissions as officers because, as they bluntly put it, 'they
did not choose to be hanged'. Meanwhile most of the
experienced American seaman were perfectly happy to
continue serving on 'privateers', private vessels which
attacked British merchant ships while steering clear of
British warships. In terms of self-interest, their decision is
all too understandable. They made handsome profits from
their raids and, by avoiding full naval conflict, ran as few
risks as possible. Arguments of the most persuasive sort
would have been needed to change their minds and
convince them to put up with the danger, the wet and
oppressive quarters and the considerably reduced prize
money for the good of the Colonies which, at that stage,
was not even a society that recognized itself as a separate
nation. Patriotism did not have the appeal that it later
would have, and there was nobody eloquent enough to
plead the navy's cause. Most seamen, therefore, stuck to the
privateers.

The navy's officers, such as they were, came from a
merchant background and lacked both the experience and
tactical expertise required for naval battles. As for the lower
ranks, press gangs were an absolute necessity. As one
captain lamented, the navy was too often crewed by 'green

country lads, many of them not clear of their seasickness', and they had to rely on foreigners and British prisoners to make up the numbers.

Lack of manpower dogged the American Navy throughout its early years and prevented it from ever really mounting an integrated naval campaign, in which task forces or fleets – rather than individual ships – would have pinned the British back to their side of the Atlantic. The situation was made even more difficult by the lack of funds, the lack of experience in building warships and Congress's inability to provide a centralized administration that could plan and coordinate both strategy and operations. A Naval Committee – later known as the Marine Committee – was appointed by Congress, but it suffered from extreme snobbery, nepotism and incompetence. Esek Hopkins, who was appointed Commodore of the Navy and whose brother was the Committee's chairman, himself dismissed the Committee as a 'pack of damn fools' and they never achieved what should have been their most essential task – to weld the individual ships into a coherent fighting force. Instead, the best captains sailed their ships all over the Atlantic, breaking up the British supply lines, harassing British commerce and foiling a total blockade by keeping the supply and communication lines open to France. They fought individually and they were picked off individually, and finally the Americans were forced to rely on French sea power after the French openly entered into alliance with them in 1778.

Perhaps, then, the sceptics might have said, 'We were right all along. The navy never stood a chance and, sure enough, it has been defeated. So, what was the point in creating it in the first place?' There can only be one way to answer them and that is to mention the name John Paul Jones. Justifiably renowned as the father of the American Navy, this Scotsman knew exactly what odds he was facing when he became first lieutenant at the salary of $20 a month in December 1775. As he himself said, so small a naval force 'had no precedent in history to make war against such a power as Great Britain'. People would be entitled to ask whether it was 'proof of madness in the first corps of sea officers to have at so critical a period launched out on the ocean'? As John Paul Jones's heroic exploits showed, the sea officers were not mad. They knew that they could disrupt the British and impede their savage attacks on the American coast. They knew that their daring and courage could vastly increase the prestige and influence of the Colonies abroad and provoke further European support for their attempts to secure autonomy, quite apart from making the war more unpopular in Britain. But their main motive was a simple one. They were tough, defiant people who wouldn't back down for anyone. The greater the odds, the more they relished the fight. And John Paul Jones was the most cussed and indomitable of them all.

In 1774, John Paul Jones could not have envisaged how his life was going to turn out. Aged twenty-five and still known by the name he was christened by, John Paul, he seemed to be on the verge of achieving what he had worked for for the last twelve years – to leave behind, once and for all, the dangers and rigours of a life at sea. As captain of the merchant ship, *Betsy*, he had entered into a profitable partnership with a merchant planter of Tobago and over two years he had amassed the, for then, considerable fortune of £2,500. At last, the prospect of retiring to become a gentleman planter in Virginia, which he had first visited in 1761, seemed a real posssibility. The future looked bright until, as he put it, he was struck by 'the greatest misfortune of my life'. In one terrible incident, which reveals a great deal about the toughness both of making a living at sea in the eighteenth century and of John Paul Jones's character, everything was thrown into jeopardy. A virulent clash broke out between the captain and crew, while the *Betsy* was docked in Tobago, over the perennially controversial subject of money. Should the crew be advanced their wages or, as John Paul Jones preferred, should the money be kept to invest in cargo for the return voyage to the British Isles? One sailor emerged as the ringleader, threatening first to lead the men off the ship, then chasing John Paul Jones to his cabin. Returning with his sword, the two men struggled and, as John Paul Jones was about to be toppled into the hold, he ran the sailor through with his sword and killed him. His first instinct was to give himself up, but on being advised that the sailor was from Tobago and so he was unlikely to get a fair trial, he left the *Betsy*, changed his name to John Paul Jones and fled to America.

Thus ended a chapter in Jones's life that began at the tender age of thirteen when he enlisted in the merchant service as an apprentice to a merchant in Whitehaven. Born in 1747 to a gardener on the Arbigland Estate in south-west Scotland, John Paul Jones grew up without money or connections but with a deep love for Scotland, for the romantic tales of Scottish resistance to British rule and, above all, for the possibilities of adventure and fame that the sea seemed to offer. From a very early age, he was transfixed by the ships plying their way along the Solway Firth between Dumfries, Whitehaven, Liverpool and the Americas. These would be his means of escape and, the moment he was apprenticed, he started working as hard as possible to improve himself both professionally and socially. In his first year at sea, he sailed first to the West Indies, then to Virginia on the brig *Friendship*, and over the following years he made several voyages to the New World, which he came to know and love. Entirely against his will, he was forced to serve on slave ships, the 'slavers' whose brutal and miserable conditions he abhorred. As soon as possible he quit this 'abominable trade' and instead served on merchant vessels, armed or otherwise, slowly improving his navigation and working his way up the ranks. In 1768, he proved his mettle when, on the return voyage from the West Indies, both the master and the mate of the little brig *John* died of fever and, aged only twenty-one, he brought it safely back to Scotland. The next year he made his maiden voyage to Jamaica as the appointed captain and with subsequent voyages to the West Indies and the captaincy of *Betsy*, both his career and his character matured and defined him as the man who would go down in the history of the country that was about to become America.

As a young man, John Paul Jones had faced many dangers and shouldered weighty responsibilities. He had navigated small ships through the brutally inhospitable conditions of the Atlantic, he had maintained discipline amongst crews of the hardest and most strong-willed sailors, and he had repeatedly made the most difficult business calculations on the cargoes that would make such arduous voyages profitable. All these experiences had left their mark on him, forging both vast reservoirs of proud independence and self-reliance, and a stubborn streak of irascibility that could flare up when he was crossed. As one of his sailors put it, he was 'sweet like a vine when he wished, but, when necessary, like a rock' and although there were obviously mitigating circumstances to the sailor's death in Tobago, John Paul Jones was not a man to back down when he was faced by adversity nor to temper his fierce determination to suit anyone's scruples.

Having added Jones to his name after the Jones family with whom his brother, William, was living, John Paul Jones settled down near his brother in Fredericksburg in Virginia and paid keen attention to the first stirrings of the War of Independence. Appointments were few and far between in 1775 at the creation of the American – or, as it was then called – the Continental Navy and John Paul Jones was neither related to, nor himself an important figure in the local community, but his experience and personality impressed the Naval Committee enough for him to be appointed first lieutenant with the task of helping fit out the 350 ton warship *Alfred*. The navy, of course, needed a flag to prove to their opponents that they were not pirates and John Paul Jones himself was the first to raise the predecessor of the Stars and Stripes – the Grand Union flag: thirteen red and white stripes, representing the thirteen Colonies, with the combined crosses of St Andrew and St George in the upper left quadrant, representing the desire for autonomy, the right for the Colonies to tax themselves without completely breaking away from the British Crown. 'I hoisted with my own hands the flag of freedom,' he proudly declared and in the spring of 1776 he took part in the American Navy's first sea battle.

It was not a particularly glorious encounter. A task force under Commodore Esek Hopkins of all five American ships raided Providence Island in the Bahamas in March to capture gunpowder and ordnance for the Continental Army and on their return, they spotted HMS *Glasgow*. Vastly superior to the British ship in firepower, the Americans, however, forfeited all their advantages by a total failure to coordinate their attacks. Instead of bringing the two columns of ships into line, each captain was left to manoeuvre as he saw fit, which allowed HMS *Glasgow* not only to escape but to inflict considerable damage. *Alfred* was holed below the waterline and its steering gear, mainmast and rigging badly cut up, Esek Hopkins was wounded, the captain of the *Cabot* was killed and, in all, ten Americans were killed and fourteen wounded to one British death and three wounded. Captain Nicholas Biddle, the captain of the *Andrew Doria*, said of the battle that 'a more imprudent ill-conducted affair never happened'.

After this ignominious opening of hostilities and to the great relief of his independent spirit, John Paul Jones was transferred to skipper the twelve-gun sloop *Providence*,

Louis XVI of France

which he led on a successful seven-week tour of the Atlantic, capturing several small vessels and disrupting the Nova Scotia fishing fleet. He repeated his successes on his next tour of the Atlantic, this time as captain of the *Alfred*, and captured four substantial British ships. Success, however, offered no protection against both the nepotism of naval appointments and the unpopularity of his style of leadership. Considered an outsider and an over-demanding taskmaster, he was replaced as captain of the *Alfred* and, for a while, not given another command. In Esek Hopkins's words, 'It is impossible to man and get these vessels together and from the number of complaints I have had . . . it will be more difficult to man vessels under his command than any other officer.'

John Paul Jones longed to be part of a task force that would cross the Atlantic and pin the British down in their own waters, but privateers still made it impossible for Congress to man enough ships and so perhaps it was with the determination to achieve single-handedly what Congress could not that, in 1777, he sailed for France in the eighteen-gun sloop *Ranger*. Burgoyne had just surrendered at Saratoga and Jones was full of optimism that he would be given command of an excellent new warship, *L'Indien*, which was being built in Amsterdam. Whether because of delays in refitting or because of pressure exerted by British partisans in Holland, Jones could not take command of *L'Indien* and, instead, he was given a mission that could have been tailor-made for his disposition – to undertake a series of raids for 'distressing the Enemies of the United States'. He set off straight away for Whitehaven and the waters where he had first taken to the sea.

The *Ranger* was a fast ship, ideal for lightning raids on the British coast, and Jones's plan was appropriately bold, to steal into Whitehaven harbour and destroy as much shipping in one night as the navy might be able to destroy in a whole year of scouring the seas. He was not, however, backed up by his crew, who preferred the Executive Officer, Lieutenant Thomas Simpson, to Jones and wanted to attack the much safer and more profitable target of British commerce. Jones enforced discipline at the point of a gun and set off in one boat, with twenty sailors, to overcome the sentries in Whitehaven's fort and spike the cannons. But instead of firing the ships, the rest of his crew went on a drinking spree, a deserter alerted the inhabitants of Whitehaven and Jones was forced to flee, having set only a few ships on fire. He then sailed north to Kirkcudbright Bay and landed on St Mary's Isle, hoping to take the Earl of Selkirk as a hostage who could be traded for the American sailors languishing in the British prison hulks, treated as pirates rather than prisoners of war. The Earl was away, but Jones's men insouciantly intruded on the Countess of Selkirk at breakfast and then headed for Northern Ireland and the prize of the twenty-gun sloop HMS *Drake*, which Jones had spotted on his way north. With great cunning, Jones drew HMS *Drake* out of Carrickfergus Bay, running up the Stars and Stripes and taking advantage of the wind, persuading them to fight. Within an hour of heavy cannon fire, HMS *Drake* surrendered and, with the frigate and the British merchantmen he had captured in tow, he returned in triumph to Brest. His reception was euphoric. Ballads were sung about the *Ranger* and its heroic captain, the American Navy's reputation blossomed and the British exchanged 228 American sailors for the prisoners Jones had taken. At last, American sailors ceased to be treated as pirates and were feared as formidable adversaries. The entire English and Scottish coast was in a state of terrible apprehension about what Jones might undertake next.

Jones couldn't wait to embark on further raiding parties and there is a sentence in one of the handbills he had printed to recruit new crews that demonstrates exactly his state of mind: 'I wish to have no connection with any ship that does not sail fast, for I intend to go in harm's way.' As was unfortunately always the case in his career, he wasn't given the command he deserved and instead of a fast warship, he took command of a sluggish old French merchantman, which he refitted and renamed *Bonhomme Richard*. Various missions were discussed, such as diversionary raids to draw attention away from a joint French and Spanish invasion of the south of England, but in the end it was decided that he would lead a task force to hunt a British convoy escorting a large number of merchantmen. The task force included three French ships and the thirty-six-gun American frigate *Alliance* under the very strange captaincy of a former French naval officer, Captain Pierre Landais. His bizarre, touchy and resentful temperament was a further hindrance that Jones had to contend with but nonetheless, as he set off from Lorient in August 1779, Jones was about to enter naval history.

For the first month of his mission, Jones led the task force round the west coast of Ireland and England, and attempted some of the acts of extreme daring that had Britain trembling. In the Firth of Forth, a British private yacht approached to ask for gunpowder to defend the coast against none other than John Paul Jones himself. With typical sang-froid, he gave them gunpowder, gathered as much information as he could about British defences and then kept one man on board to pilot him into Leith harbour and fire all the ships there. When the yacht had pulled away, John Paul Jones nonchalantly asked the pilot what the news was. 'Why,' the pilot burst out, 'that rebel and pirate Jones is off the coast and he ought to be hanged.' John Paul Jones calmly replied, 'I am Paul Jones' and, as the pilot begged for mercy on his knees, he simply laughed and assured him that he wouldn't be harmed. Storms intervened to protect Leith and meanwhile Landais was behaving ever more erratically, refusing to obey Jones's orders and going off on his own. But at sunset on

23 September 1779, Jones finally spotted the forty-one ship convoy protected by HMS *Serapis* off Flamborough Head on the Yorkshire coast.

The British ship was newer, faster, more manoeuvrable and better armed than the *Bonhomme Richard*. As Jones ran up the Stars and Stripes, the ships opened fire and two of Jones's eighteen-pounders exploded immediately, killing many of the gunners and putting the biggest guns out of action. It was instantly clear that the only chance Jones had against such speed and firepower was to get right up to the *Serapis* and board it – obviously, enormously risky and difficult to achieve, since the *Serapis* would be trying to keep its distance. Both ships jockeyed for position, the British trying to go broadside, Jones trying to keep them close. With supreme skill, Jones suddenly took advantage of a burst of wind to rush ahead of the *Serapis* and then lock the two ships together. 'Well done, my brave lads,' he shouted, 'we have got her now!' and grappling hooks gripped the *Serapis* in a fatal embrace. For two hours, at point-blank range, an unforgettable battle raged. The British could not get away and the American sharpshooters high in *Bonhomme Richard*'s rigging scoured the decks with grenades and gunfire. At the same time the British eighteen-pounders wiped out most of the American cannons and devastated the American ship, thundering round after round into its shattered frame. To make things even worse, Landais suddenly had the *Alliance* open broadside fire on the *Bonhomme Richard*, his lethal jealousy driving him to try and finish Jones off and claim victory for himself.

As fires broke out all over the ship and his gunners died in droves, Jones took over one of the nine-pounders on the quarterdeck and, to his incredulity, heard his chief gunner shout out, 'Quarter! quarter! for God's sake!' His ship may have been taking in water, his crew decimated and, for the last two hours, he may have endured a firefight that would have driven other men insane, but nothing would have induced John Paul Jones to surrender. So when Pearson, HMS *Serapis*'s Commander, shouted back, 'Do you ask for quarter?' Jones uttered the famous words, 'I have not begun to fight.' This indomitable will-power won the day. Firing again and again at *Serapis*'s mainmast, Jones finally brought it down and Pearson could stand the carnage no longer. He surrendered and Jones left the shattered *Bonhomme Richard* for the last time. It sank the next day and, after ten days' tortuous sailing, Jones brought the *Serapis* and 500 prisoners into the Texel in Holland.

This incredible triumph and Jones's peerless heroism were the talk of Europe. Louis XVI awarded him the Order of Military Merit and Congress passed a vote of thanks for his services to the Flag. But, in a sad irony, it was both the pinnacle and the end of Jones's naval career. He arrived back in Philadelphia after an appallingly stormy crossing in 1781 but was given no further commands and Congress sold off the last warship, none other than the *Alliance*, in 1785. Nor was he promoted to Flag rank. On the recommendation of Thomas Jefferson, he was made Admiral of Russia's Black Sea Fleet, under Catherine the Great, but politics meant he never had more than a tactical role on land. He returned to France and the Revolution prevented him from leaving. In 1792, aged forty-five, he died a pauper's death in Paris and was buried in an unmarked grave in the Protestant cemetery. A hundred years later his grave was discovered and his body re-interred in a specially built mausoleum in the Naval Academy at Annapolis in Maryland, an institution which his example had done so much to help establish. Now there is a museum at his birthplace and, once again, people can admire the astonishing exploits of this 'illustrious hero of the American Revolution'.